Your
Memory
For Life!

Your Memory For Life!

Develop, Improve and Retain
Lifetime Memory Skills

Michael M. Gruneberg
Douglas J. Herrmann

BLANDFORD

The authors would like to thank Jan Gruneberg and
Tony and Carrie Bickard for their useful comments on an
earlier draft of the book.

A Blandford Book
First published in the UK 1997 by Blandford
a Cassell imprint
Cassell plc,
Wellington House
125 Strand
London WC2R 0BB

Distributed in the United States by Sterling Publishing Co., Inc.,
387 Park Avenue South, New York, NY 10016-8810

A Cataloguing-in-Publication Data entry for this title is available from the British
Library.

ISBN   0-7137-2630 X

Designed and Typeset by Ben Cracknell Studios

Printed and bound in Great Britain by Creative Print and Design Wales, Ebbw Vale

Contents

Introduction

Many popular books have been written on memory. Almost all of these tell readers how to improve their memory; and they all give advice that works. Thus, while this book will also show you how you can use memory aids and memory devices to improve your memory for names and faces, foreign languages, ideas, examinations and many other useful tasks, it does much more than this.

It looks at a large number of areas where many people are concerned about their memories and gives up-to-date advice on how best to deal with the problems they face. For example, we look at memory as we get older, memory in children, memory of eyewitnesses in a court case, memory for examinations and memory following brain damage. The book also looks at topics such as health and memory and the ways in which emotions and stress affect memory. It shows the reader how to improve his or her ability to keep appointments and find keys as well as how best to overcome memory block. The final chapter is in the form of an owner's manual and explains how your memory works and how best to look after it.

We have called this book *Your Memory For Life* for two reasons. First, the memory skills it describes can be useful to you for the rest of your life, although you may not need to use them every day. Second, the skills apply to a wide variety of real life situations, not just to tricks or games of the mind. Our hope is, therefore, that you will indeed find this book useful for life.

MMG/DJH
Swansea, UK/Indiana, USA
1997

Your Memory is Better than You Think

Most people do not realize that their memory is better than they think, but this chapter will show you how much better your memory can be. One way of doing this is to look at the way images improve memory. Let us suppose, for example, that you wanted to remember that the Spanish for *bread* is *pan*. You can remember this easily by imagining a *pan* full of *bread*. Simple images like this can help to make your ability to remember better than it is normally.

NOW TEST YOURSELF

Below is a list of words that have been arranged in pairs. Test how easy it is for you to remember which words go together by the picturing method. For example, to remember that **alligator** goes with **flag**, make a picture in your mind's eye to link **alligator** and **flag** – perhaps you might picture an **alligator** with a **flag** sticking out of its head. For every pair of words below, make a picture. Make sure you make a good picture for each pair before you move on to the next pair.

Alligator	Flag	Fish	Tree	Shoe	Stone
Dog	Chalk	House	Car	Mouse	Chair
Stamp	Pencil	Hen	Shirt	Carpet	Cow
Book	Cat	Hand	Coffee	Window	Gate

Now turn to the next page.

Below is a list of words. Each word is the first word of the pairs you have just learned. See how many of the words that went with the words below you can remember. Turn back for the correct answers *after* you have written out all the words you can remember.

Alligator	_____
Dog	_____
Stamp	_____
Book	_____
Fish	_____
House	_____
Hen	_____
Hand	_____
Shoe	_____
Mouse	_____
Carpet	_____
Window	_____

Most people get more than half correct if they used images, but less than half if they did not use images. What's more, the effect of images often gets better with practice. If you did not do well on this exercise, don't worry! How well you do has nothing to do with intelligence – it just means you may not be 'built' to use pictures/images. Don't give up; it often comes with practice.

Recognizing Words

As the previous section showed, your memory can be much better than you thought. The problem seems to be less a lack of storage space than a matter of getting material out of store.

NOW TEST YOURSELF

To show how great your ability to store information is, read through the following list of words, at about the rate of one every two seconds. Even though the list is long, try to read it through to the end in one go. We think you will be amazed at what happens next.

1. Refinery	31. Mirage
2. Abbess	32. Albino
3. Sahara	33. Tiddlywinks
4. Tartan	34. Bedouin
5. Helmsman	35. Limpet
6. Ignition	36. Tirade
7. Polyp	37. Reverie
8. Milliner	38. Archway
9. Teacup	39. Carnage
10. Artichoke	40. Rostrum
11. Hailstone	41. Zealot
12. Gangrene	42. Elixir
13. Mucous	43. Giraffe
14. Galleon	44. Affray
15. Torso	45. Hawthorn
16. Panacea	46. Parsonage
17. Impotence	47. Autocrat
18. Harpsichord	48. Plasma
19. Baton	49. Vampire
20. Dualism	50. Cauldron
21. Heraldry	51. Rabies
22. Claret	52. Porthole
23. Keyhole	53. Bigot
24. Seesaw	54. Toadstool
25. Faggot	55. Geyser
26. Lintel	56. Wallop
27. Pagoda	57. Sinus
28. Termite	58. Halibut
29. Scarecrow	59. Gizzard
30. Belfry	60. Whalebone

Now turn to the next page.

Below is a list of ten words. Five of these words were on the list you have just learned (old words), five of them are new. Just say of each word whether it is new or old.

Refinery
Mimosa
Mirage
Poultice
Felony
Carnage
Rabies
Turbine
Claret
Mohair

Now turn back to see which words are on the first list.

If you correctly identified the five old words as old and the five new words as new, you can assume that you have stored all sixty words in the original list. If you made one mistake, you have scored 80 per cent, two mistakes, 60 per cent, three mistakes, 40 per cent and so on. Many people score 60 per cent or more, showing that a huge amount of material has been stored. Of course, if you were asked to recall the words you had read, you would not recall nearly so many, which suggests that the problem is basically one of getting the words out of store, rather than of storing the words in the first place.

In summary, the point of the demonstrations in this chapter is to show you that your memory really is much better than you think. In the rest of the book we will show you how you can help yourself to have a better memory in a wide range of situations.

Improving Your Memory with Memory Aids

In the last chapter we saw how good your memory is at storing information. We also saw that if we use images to picture new words together, remembering new pairs of words becomes much easier. The use of imagery, picturing words together, is at the heart of many memory aids.

The Method of Loci

The use of imagery as an aid to memory was known to the ancient Greeks. The Greek orator Simonides is said to have invented memory aids almost by accident. He was giving a speech at a banquet when he was called outside by two messengers. When he went outside, the banquet hall collapsed, killing everyone inside. Not only were the guests killed, they were so badly mangled that their relatives could not identify them. Simonides, however, had used imagery to picture where each guest had been sitting, and so he was able to identify the bodies for the grieving relatives. The relatives were comforted, and Simonides's place in history was secured for all time. It truly is an ill wind that blows no body any good!

The method Simonides invented – the method of loci – can help learners to remember all sorts of things, including people, by using picturing to associate a place with an object or person. The first thing a learner has to do is 'fix' a number of familiar places in his or her mind's eye. For example, think of your bedroom. In the centre of your bedroom might be your bed, next to the bed is a table, next to the table is a chair, next to the chair is a dressing-table, and so on. Go round your bedroom clockwise, picturing in your mind ten 'places', such as your bed, the table and so on. You don't need to choose your bedroom of course. Anywhere you can picture, in order, ten places will do.

When you want to learn a new set of words, say Duck, Hat, Cheese and so on, what you need to do is this. Picture the first new word you want to learn on the first 'place' in your bedroom, in this example you might picture a Duck laying an egg on your Bed. The second word to be learned, Hat, you might picture on the second place, the Table; the third word Cheese, spread over the third place, your Chair, and so on.

NOW TEST YOURSELF

To show you how good the method of loci is, try learning this list of ten words. Before you do so, however, make sure you can picture ten places in your bedroom, going clockwise round your bedroom. Now remember the following ten words by placing them in turn on the 'places' you have pictured in your bedroom. Picture the places and the objects together as vividly as you can.

1.	Rattlesnake	6.	Piano
2.	Ice-cream	7.	Ink
3.	Computer	8.	Popcorn
4.	Banana	9.	Shirt
5.	Book	10.	Handcuffs

Now cover the list with a piece of paper. Write out all ten words. Then check to see how many you got right.

Most people get about seven right. If you have not done as well as this, don't worry. It almost always gets better with practice.

The Peg or Hook System

The method of loci is a good way of improving your ability to remember things, but it has one limitation: in order to remember, say, the sixth word, you have to start at the beginning and go through the pictures until you come to what you are looking for. The peg or hook system allows you to remember words in any order. It also works by using imagery to link up a new word to an image. Before you can use this system you have to learn a very simple poem.

One is Bun	Six is Sticks
Two is Shoe	Seven is Heaven
Three is Tree	Eight is Gate
Four is Door	Nine is Wine
Five is Hive	Ten is Hen

Make sure you have learned this poem well before you go on. Say it to yourself twice correctly with your eyes closed.

To use the peg system picture the first new word you want to learn with the first word in the poem, the second new word with the second word in the poem and so on. If the first three new words to learn were Dog, Plate and Arrow, you would picture a Dog eating a Bun (first peg word), a Shoe (second peg word) on a Plate, and an Arrow hitting a Tree (third peg word).

NOW TEST YOURSELF

Learn the words below using the peg word method. Picture each new word with the peg word it goes with.

1. Pig	6. Window
2. Stone	7. Tooth
3. Fish	8. Lizard
4. Clock	9. Grass
5. Car	10. Prison

Now turn over and complete the questions.

What is the third word you were given? _____

What is the fifth word you were given? _____

What is the second word you were given? _____

What is the eighth word you were given? _____

What is the first word you were given? _____

What is the fourth word you were given? _____

What is the ninth word you were given? _____

What is the tenth word you were given? _____

What is the sixth word you were given? _____

What is the seventh word you were given? _____

Turn back to check your answers. Most people get about seven out of ten correct. If you got fewer than this, don't worry; you probably need to practice more and to make sure you can remember the poem. Try making up lists of ten words and using the peg system to remember them. If you find it difficult to make a picture, try making a sentence that links the two pairs of words together. A large number of scientific experiments has shown that the peg method helps most people to remember, so it is worth persevering with.

If you are like most people, you will be quite impressed with yourself and the ability of your memory by now. One great advantage of using memory aids is that they give you the confidence that you can remember things if you want to. The question is, what are you doing now that you didn't do before? The answer is that you are using imagery to link words together more strongly than normal, so that as soon as you have one word, it is easy to remember what it is linked to. You are using a memory aid as an effective method of remembering in a systematic way.

So now you know how to remember ten words in any order. 'That's very useful,' you might think. 'I often need to know a list of words, like Pig, Stone, Fish, Clock – I *don't* think!' It is valid to question how useful memory aides are, because remembering things for the sake of it does seem to be a complete waste of time. Yet there are occasions when remembering lists of things can be extremely useful.

Mental filing system

One such situation is the so-called 'filing system' use. If, for example, you are lying awake at night and ideas occur to you that you want to remember in the morning but you are too tired or lazy to get up and write them down, the mental filing system comes into its own. Suppose, for example, in the middle of the night you have a great idea to see if:

1. Adding a *gear* will help your machine
2. Turning your *machine upside down*
3. Asking *Uncle Willy* to pay for the gear
4. Adjusting machine sales on the *spreadsheet* to account for increased sales
5. Setting a *date* for the launch of the new machine.

You first have to translate each idea into something you can picture, so

1. You picture a *gear*
2. You picture your *machine* upside down
3. You picture your *Uncle Willy*
4. You picture your *spreadsheet*
5. You picture a *bunch of dates*.

The next stage is to link each idea to the pegs you have learned, so

1. You picture, for example, your *gear* crushing a *bun* (one)
2. You picture, for example, your *machine* cleaning out *shoes* (two)
3. You picture, for example, your *Uncle Willy* stuck up a *tree* (three)
4. You picture, for example, your *spreadsheet* nailed to a *door* (four)
5. You picture, for example, feeding *dates* to bees in a *hive* (five).

Exactly the same mental filing system is useful if you are travelling to a meeting and cannot write ideas down. If you are driving a car, for example, you simply make your ideas into something that you can picture, then link them to the pegs of the poem. Exactly the same method of remembering applies when you are travelling except that it is a good idea to rehearse the links mentally from time to time, and especially just before you need to use them.

Of course you don't need to use the mental filing system very often. If an idea that you get at night is of vital importance, it is probably better to get up and write it down. But often good ideas do come to us at night, and we think, mistakenly, that we will easily remember them in the morning. It is this kind of idea that is extremely useful to put in the mental filing system. Often ideas look a lot less brilliant in the morning than when you first thought about them during the night – but that is not the fault of the filing system.

NOW TEST YOURSELF

Here is another exercise to show you that this method works equally well with people. Try to remember the following famous people using exactly the same method. Imagine the first person eating a bun, the second person throwing a shoe up in the air, etc.

1. Sean Connery (James Bond)
2. Albert Einstein
3. Marilyn Monroe
4. Winston Churchill
5. John F. Kennedy
6. John Lennon
7. Nelson Mandela
8. George Washington
9. Abraham Lincoln
10. Adolf Hitler

On the next page. Write down all the people you can remember. Write down as many as possible before looking back to find the correct answers.

Fill in the correct names in the list below

1. _____
2. _____
3. _____
4. _____
5. _____
6. _____
7. _____
8. _____
9. _____
10. _____

Obviously in scoring this, you cannot be expected to remember anyone you did not know. You should therefore expect to get about 70 per cent of the people you actually know!

In summary, this chapter has looked at some of the classical memory aids, such as the method of loci and the peg system. These have been shown to help most people to remember objects in a dramatically improved way. The method used - imagery, is at the heart of a number of different memory aids, but the method of loci and the peg system also have a practical use in acting as a mental filing system, when you can't write your ideas down.

Some Everyday Uses of Memory Aids

The method of loci and the peg system can, of course, be used for remembering any set of objects or facts, including for example, the points to be made for an after-dinner speech. In fact, the use of the method of loci was developed by the Greeks and Romans just for this purpose. They used to deliver long speeches by using memory aids to remember the points they wished to make. And so can you. If you wish to use memory aids to help you remember a speech, you should make key points. For example, if your speech was about the arguments over abolishing capital punishment, you might list the first four main points as:

1. The possibility of *mistakes* that cannot be *rectified*.

2. Evidence for *eyewitnesses* making *mistakes*.

3. The State needs to *deter* crime.

4. *Costs* of keeping a person in prison for forty years.

Again you will need to make a picture of each point. You might picture 'mistakes' by picturing Adam eating the forbidden fruit. Eyewitnesses making a mistake might be pictured by imagining an eyewitness pointing to the judge instead of the defendant when asked to say who committed a crime. To picture the State deterring crime, picture everyone having their heads cut off, and for the cost of keeping a person in prison, imagine handing over your lottery winnings to a prison governor to keep a prisoner well looked after. As you can see, with a bit of effort, more or less everything can be made into a picture. How, then, are these pictures linked to the peg words or places?

1 Mistake – Adam eating the forbidden fruit. It is easy to picture Adam eating an apple in a *bun*.

2. Eyewitness mistakes – witness pointing at a judge. It is easy to picture the judge throwing a *shoe* at the witness.

3. Deterrence – cutting off everyone's heads. You can picture a large number of heads pinned to a *tree*.

4. Cost – giving your lottery winnings away. You can picture the prison governor nailing the money to the prison *door*.

As you can see from the examples just given, the construction of images is likely to be time-consuming and sometimes complicated, even though, in the end, the effort is likely to pay off in a better memory of the points you wish to make. It is much simpler in many situations simply to write down the key words on a piece of paper, and these key words are almost certainly going to be enough, in a well-prepared speech, to trigger off what you want to say, without you seeming to be reading. Even if you do decide to remember the key points using memory aids, it is probably better to write the key points down and leave them in front of you anyway – just in case you forget an association under the stress of giving a speech. Having the list of key points in front of you will make it easier for you to relax and make it less likely you will need the list in any case.

Remembering Jokes

When making after-dinner speeches, speakers often like to tell jokes, and this is one area where memory aids come into their own. This is because most people are hopeless at remembering jokes. How often have you said: 'I've heard it before but I can't remember how it ends'? The memory principle is the same as before. Isolate the keyword in the punch line of the joke, then associate the first keyword with one – bun and so on. Here are five jokes:

Joke 1 – The Guillotine Joke

Three men from England, a carpenter, a soldier and an Oxford professor, were caught trying to help a nobleman to escape during the French Revolution. They were all condemned to die by the guillotine and were all brought to the place of execution. The first to be placed on the block was the carpenter. He was placed face down, the guillotine was released, but when it was about an inch from his neck, the blade stopped suddenly. The crowd gasped and declared it was a miracle from God and the carpenter was sent on his way.

Next, the soldier faced the guillotine. His hands were bound, but before he could be placed on the block, he declared that he was braver than the carpenter and would meet his death facing the blade. His wish was granted. He was placed face up on the block and the blade released. Amazingly, just before the blade reached his throat, it suddenly stopped. Again, the crowd shouted, 'it's a miracle from God, let him go'. So he was released.

Finally, it came to the turn of the Oxford professor. 'I'm as brave as the soldier,' he said. 'I, too, want to face the blade and you don't need to bind my hands, I will not resist!' So his wish was granted. He was placed facing the blade, but just as the blade was about to be released, he waved his arms in the air, shouting, 'Wait a minute, I've worked out what's causing it to stick!'

1.   One – Bun – Guillotine

Imagine a guillotine cutting a bun in half.

Joke 2 – The Ice Hockey Joke

James Smith was mad about ice hockey. He went to a priest one day and asked if they played ice hockey in Heaven. The priest promised to find out the next time he prayed. A week later James went to Sunday service and the priest called him aside at the end. 'I've got through to Heaven,' he said. 'There is good news and bad news and good news. The good news is that there is ice hockey in Heaven and they have three teams, a top team, a middle team and a poor team. The bad news is that you will be playing goal tender a week next Thursday! The good news is that you are going straight into the top team!'

2.   Two – Shoe – Hockey stick

Imagine hitting a shoe with a hockey stick.

Joke 3 – The Aeroplane Joke

Two experts in statistics were on a plane from London to New York. Half way over the Atlantic, one of the engines fell off. The pilot's voice came over the intercom. 'This is your pilot speaking. One of the engines has just fallen off. There's no problem as the plane can fly with three engines. However, we will be an hour late arriving at New York.'

Two hours later there was an explosion on the other wing, and a second engine fell off. 'This is your pilot speaking, we have lost another engine, but there is no need to worry, the plane can fly with two engines. However, we will be two hours late arriving in New York.' Within a few minutes a further explosion rocked the plane and a third engine fell off. 'This is your captain speaking. I have to tell you that a third engine has fallen off. However, there is no need to worry since these planes can fly and land on only one engine. However, we will be four hours late arriving in New York.' The first statistics expert said to his friend, 'I hope the fourth engine doesn't fall off, or we'll be up here all night!'

3.   Three – Tree

Imagine an aeroplane crashing into a tree.

Joke 4 – The Old Man Joke

An old man went to see a priest. 'Father,' he said. 'I am eighty-five years old, and last week I slept with an attractive seventeen-year-old girl!'

'Did you?' said the priest.

'Yes, five times,' said the man.

'Did you?' said the priest.

'Yes, in one night,' said the man.

'Are you married?' asked the priest.

'No, Father.'

'That is terrible,' said the Priest. 'You must say twenty-five Hail Mary's.'

'I can't do that, Father.'

'Why not?' asked the Priest.

'Because I'm Jewish,' said the man.

'Well, if you are Jewish, why are you telling me?' asked the Priest.

'Why not? I'm telling *everybody*!' said the man.

    4.   Door – Old man banging on a door

Imagine an old man banging on a door to get inside.

Joke 5 – The Rabbit Joke

There were three rabbits, Foot, Foot-Foot and Foot-Foot-Foot. One day they all got into Farmer Brown's cabbage patch and gorged themselves. They had eaten so much that when they got home that night they became very ill and called the doctor, but before the doctor arrived, Foot died. The doctor warned Foot-Foot and Foot-Foot-Foot against the danger of eating cabbage, but a month later Farmer Brown was again away, so they gorged themselves again on cabbage, and again, having eaten too much, became violently ill. The doctor was called again, and when he arrived he was furious. 'How could you do this?' he asked 'When you already have one Foot in the grave?'

    5.   Hive – Rabbits

Imagine rabbits trying to eat a bee hive.

NOW TEST YOURSELF

*Without looking back, see how many of the jokes
you can remember.*

What was joke:

3. _____

5. _____

2. _____

4. _____

1. _____

Most people can remember all the jokes using this method, and can remember many more using the extended peg system (see page 26), but if you want to remember them for a long time, you must refresh your memory periodically by going through them again.

The Story Method

In fact, you do not need to use either the method of loci or the peg method in order to use imagery. You can simply link all the words you want to remember together in pictures, one after the other. Suppose the words you want to remember are Dog, Car, House, Snow and so on. First, you picture say a Dog chasing a Car. Then you picture a Car crashing into a House. Then you picture a House covered in Snow and so on. Each word automatically leads to the next one. It is a highly effective method of remembering, provided you make vivid pictures to link the words together, but if you forget one link, the rest of the words are likely to be forgotten. If you used this method to remember the speech on capital punishment, you would picture Adam talking to eyewitnesses, the eyewitness then points out the judge, the judge then cuts off the heads of everyone around, a head then 'hands over' lottery money to the prison governor and so on.

The peg system you have learned only goes up to ten. However, if you want, you can extend the number of jokes, or anything else you want to remember, to many thousands! But be warned, jokes fade, even with memory systems, if you do not refresh them by going over them from time to time.

Of course, what works for memorizing jokes can be used for lots of things you want to know. The peg system can be used for remembering information you need to know at work; you can even use it to learn facts relevant to a hobby.

A lot of people feel very self-conscious when they first use the peg system. This is normal. People usually do feel a little odd when they do something they have not done before. For example, a lot of people feel the images are silly. But stick with it. People who do, find their feelings of self-consciousness and silliness disappear.

The Number–letter System

The number–letter system can be used to help with remembering numbers. Because numbers are basically meaningless, they are often very difficult to remember. Many of us have had embarrassing failures to remember our bank PIN numbers or telephone numbers of friends. The number–letter system can help solve this kind of problem. First you have to learn letter equivalents of numbers:

1. = t (There is one down stroke in the letter t)
2. = n (There are two down strokes in the letter n)
3. = m (There are three down strokes in the letter m)
4. = r (The last letter of four is r!)
5. = l (The Roman number 50 is L)
6. = sh (The word six has a SH (sort of) sound)
7. = k (The number 7 is embedded in the letter k)
8. = f (when handwritten, f looks like 8)
9. = p (9 is a 'p' the wrong way around!)
0. = s (s is the first sound in zero!)

You must learn these before you go on. In order to remember numbers, you translate a number into its equivalent letter. So 141 is TRT (T=1, R=4, T=1). You now use any vowels you like to make TRT into a word. So TRT could be TART. The number 121, TNT could be TINT or TENT. You use vowels in any way you like to make up a word by filling in between the letter equivalents of numbers. By this method, 19 is TP, which could be TOP, TAP or TIP, and 35 is ML, which could be MEAL, MILE, MOLE and so on.

You can use this system to remember your PIN number. Suppose the number is 2852, which would be NFLN. This could be NO FEELIN'!

Similarly, you can make a word or words in order to remember someone's phone number. Be warned, however, that it sometimes takes time to make up a good word or phrase, and if the phrase is not very good, you can forget it. You really do need to practise using the number–letter system for remembering long strings of numbers. You should use this method, therefore, only when it is important to learn a particular number, such as a new telephone number of a friend. After a while, you will remember the number without needing the help of a memory aid, but it is often useful to begin with.

There are times when it is important to remember only two numbers, such as the date of your wedding anniversary or your partner's birthday! One of the present authors uses the number–letter system to remember that his wife's birthday is on 19 January. He could never remember whether it was on the 19th or 20th, with sometimes unfortunate consequences. He used the number–letter system to translate 19 into TP and to make the word TOP to which he added 'less' in order to remember better! Then he imagined his wife topless on her birthday! He has never forgotten his wife's birthday since he adopted this method.

One use of the number–letter system is in remembering car licence plates. In Britain number plates usually take the form of a letter, indicating the year of registration, followed by three digits, followed by three letters. For example, a number plate might be K239 FSL. In order to remember this, it should be remembered that in the UK, the last three letters are probably the most important. So the first thing to do is make something meaningful out of these three letters. For example, FSL could be *FOSSIL*, where you make a meaningful word or phrase out of the letters, or you might have the phrase Fast Stupid Liar. Having remembered the letters, turn the numbers into letters, so 2 3 9 becomes N M P. This might translate into *N*ame *P*late (forget the last part of the word). Then try to remember the registration letter, which is usually quite easy. In the United States WMU374 is a number plate in Maryland. WMU could stand for West Maryland University; 374 = m k r = *MY KAR*.

Extending the Peg System

One of the main uses of the number–letter system is that it allows you to generate as many pegs for the peg system as you need. As you know, the one-bun system gives you up to ten items to remember, but the number–letter system increases the number of pegs by translating numbers into letters. For example,

   11   becomes tt – e.g., TOOT
   12   becomes tn – e.g., TIN
   13   becomes tm – e.g., TEAM
   14   becomes tr – e.g., TEAR – and so on
   121 becomes tnt – e.g., TENT

In order to remember that, say, Alligator is the 121st word you want to remember, you picture an alligator in a tent and so on.

It has to be said that for most purposes, it is not clear that the extended peg system is going to be terribly useful in everyday life, but there are some obvious uses, such as in remembering jokes. We saw earlier how jokes can be successfully remembered by using the peg system, and we come across a large number of jokes in our lifetime. We usually hear them when we cannot write them down, so using the peg and extended peg system is really an ideal way of remembering a very large number of jokes, if that is something you want to do!

Actors Learning Lines

Some actors use memory aids to help them remember their lines. The famous memory man Harry Lorayne has shown that an actor can learn lines quickly using adaptations of the imagery method. Interestingly, though, studies have shown that even though actors know about memory aids, and use them in a few restricted situations, they are not normally used for this purpose. Actors usually learn their lines by getting deeply into the character of the part they are to play, so that they can 'feel' what a character would say in any particular situation. The actor then 'fine-tunes' the actual dialogue. One reason for taking this approach is that the speed of learning lines is secondary to learning them in such a way that the actor gives depth to the part. It is not only what is said, but also how it is said that is important.

Of course, there is no good evidence we know of that using mnemonic strategies would prevent an actor from thinking deeply about the character who was saying the words. It is possible that, as in many other spheres of learning, the distrust of quick methods of learning is misplaced. It is also true that in some situations, when what is to be learned is pretty meaningless, actors have been reported as using imagery memory aids to remember their lines. Moreover, some individuals do find it difficult to remember lines using conventional acting approaches, and for such actors, memory aids might well be useful as mental crutches until the lines are learned and they can then get 'into' the part.

In summary, this chapter has shown you how you can improve your memory with memory aids. For most people they work very well, but don't worry if they don't work for you. Nothing works for everyone, and whether you can use memory aids or not has nothing to do with intelligence. Memory aids are best used in a very limited way, to remember ideas or jokes when you cannot write them down, or to help you remember points you want to make in speeches, or your friend's telephone number or your wife's birthday.

Remembering Faces and Learning a Foreign Language

Two of the most important ways in which memory aids can really help in overcoming common problems are in remembering names and learning a foreign language. There is a great deal that can be done to help you with both of these problems.

Remembering Names and Faces

Forgetting the name of someone you have met but whom you feel you should remember is a common problem for people of all ages, but this forgetfulness increases as we get older. It is always embarrassing when it happens because, if we forget someone's name, the implication is that the forgotten person is not important to us. However, help is at hand for people of all ages!

The method used to improve memory for faces and names is similar to that described in the last chapter: you use imagery to picture the face and the name together. Suppose, for example, you met a Mr Fox. The way you remember who Mr Fox is, is to take a feature of his face, such as a nose, and turn it into a fox-like nose. You then picture this as vividly as you can, so when you see the person again, you will remember his 'fox-like' nose! If you want to remember a Mr Green, imagine his nose painted a vivid, luminous green.

If the someone has a name that does not mean anything, like Sykes or Lucas or Herrmann, you need to make a meaningful word out of the name. Sykes might become 'socks' or 'sex'. Lucas might become 'look us' or 'lick us' and Herrmann might become 'airman'. You might imagine Mr Sykes with socks covering his large ears, or Mr Lucas looking at you with his enormous eyes or licking you like a dog, or Mr Herrmann wearing airman's goggles.

Some names are very common – Smith or Jones, for instance. To help, you might imagine any Mr Smith as a blacksmith and whenever you meet someone called Smith, you can use this picture. Often you can think of a friend or a famous person with the same name, and then you can imagine the new person you are introduced to being punched on the nose by the famous person. So Mr Jones might be slapped on his face by the famous singer Tom Jones, and so on. If that fails you can always go back to the substitute method described above.

Most people find that the method helps to increase their memory for names and faces by anything up to 80 per cent, and the method is effective for children as young as five and for elderly people. Indeed, the method is so effective that it is used to help brain-damaged people to remember those around them. Some individuals find that thinking of a substitute name or a picture linking the face and name is difficult, but if a helper does this for a disabled person, then his or her memory for names and faces can be greatly improved (see chapter 16).

Of course, this method is not for everyone. Some people feel odd creating images in this way, and some people are not particularly good at creating images, although they usually improve with practice. However, even if you are not good at making images, using the method involves doing two things that help you with learning the name anyway. First, you have to pay attention to the name, and second, you have to look carefully at the face. In many instances it is a failure to do these things that leads to a poor memory for names and faces in the first place!

NOW TEST YOURSELF

Until you try it you probably don't think that this system will work, so below are ten names and faces for you to remember using this method. Picture the faces and names together as vividly as you can. Then cover the pictures with a piece of paper. How many can you remember?

Ms White

Ms Beach

Mr Blair

Ms Singer

Mr Bird

Mr McGregor

Ms Piper

Mr Thomas

Ms Hart

Now turn to the next page.

Put as many names to the faces as you can. Do not look back at the answers until you are finished.

So many studies have shown that the imagery method improves name–face learning that the question is not 'Does it work?' but rather, 'How should I use it?' This is a very important question because if you use it when you should not, it will not work for you and you will soon give up using it at all. First, our advice is to use it only when you need to. In many situations it is completely pointless to learn someone's name because there is a high probability that you will never meet him or her again, and if you do and that person is likely to be important to you, then you can learn his or her name on the second occasion. These methods are best regarded as tools to be used when they are likely to be needed rather than new toys to be played with all the time. After all, if you buy a chain saw, you generally use it to cut trees, not to cut everything in sight that could be cut!

As soon as you try to use the method at the first party you go to, you will see why the advice we give is so useful. Most people find it is quite impossible to conduct a sensible conversation and to make a vivid image linking the name to the face at the same time. Of course, the more you practise, the better you will get, but in situations like parties, it does seem a considerable waste of time to try to remember the names of all the people you meet. If you do meet someone whose name you want to remember, in order to avoid the problem of holding a conversation and making an image at the same time, excuse yourself to get another drink or go to the toilet, and then make the image. Once you have made the images of people you want to remember, it will help your memory even more if you mentally picture and think about the name and face from time to time after the first meeting.

We suggest that the imagery method is best used for remembering people who are likely to be important to you, unless, of course, you enjoy doing it for its own sake. However, there are professions and situations where it is important to remember names and faces. Here, obviously, it is necessary to use the method more efficiently. One such profession is in salesmanship, where it is vitally important that you remember the name of your customers. The same rules apply as before. Look carefully at a face for a particular feature, then find a substitute name if needed and associate this as vividly as you can with the face. It is sensible to practise making name–face associations before you have to use them, and this can be done by using photographs in newspapers, magazines and so on. It is still the case, however, that until you become very skilled and can make good associations in a second or two, you should wait until the interview is over before trying to make an association, or you will disrupt the on-going conversation.

If you have to remember a number of names from a particular organization, you can use the peg system to help you. Suppose you meet Mr McGregor, Mrs Booker, Mr Avery, Dr Wall, Mr Ivan Smith, Mrs Fisher and Mr John Smith. You might picture:

1. Rob Roy McGregor eating a bun.
2. Mrs Booker putting a book into a shoe.
3. An aviary with a tree in the middle and Mr Avery sitting in the tree.
4. A doctor with a white coat trying to open a door in a wall.
5. A blacksmith looking like Mr Smith, but with a terrible look on his face (Ivan the Terrible!) smashing a beehive with a hammer.
6. Mrs Fisher fishing with a stick instead of a rod.
7. A blacksmith with wings, in heaven, who looks like *John* F. Kennedy.

As with points you make for speeches, you should always write down the names of people you need to know. If you don't forget them, fine, but if you do, you can always look them up. Almost always, once you are given the name, you can remember what they look like, so before going to visit a firm, you will know who is who, even if you meet them unexpectedly in the corridor. There is evidence that the more you know about an individual before you meet him or her, the easier it is to remember the name and face. This may happen because we build up a picture of what an individual looks like from, say, the voice on the telephone, and even when there is a great mismatch between what you expect and what the person looks like, the effect of knowing about someone makes it easy to identify that person when you meet. Both the present authors have been involved in organizing conferences for more than three hundred people, and because of the considerable correspondence that was conducted with virtually every individual before the conference, almost all the delegates were easily recognized and could be named during the conference. The process is one of: 'John Green – so that's what he looks like. He doesn't look much considering his reputation!' The lesson is clear. If you are going to visit an organization of any kind, get as much information as you can about all the people you are going to meet. You may find that you don't need to use images to remember names and faces if you know all about the people beforehand.

The critical importance of remembering names and faces in some situations should not be underestimated. Two obvious examples are police work and teaching. In police work, remembering names and faces is critical in searching for suspects. In teaching, remembering names and faces is critical in giving the child or student the feeling that he or she is significant to the teacher or professor. However, there are almost no situations, from nursing to running a business, where learning whom you are working with and whom you are working for is not important. The methods we have shown you, therefore, are likely to be of considerable value, provided you do not overuse them. If you do, it will seem too much effort to make it worthwhile, and you will abandon what is often a useful method in a range of situations.

A major problem of remembering names and faces arises in social situations where you block on the name. You know it, but it just won't come back. Overcoming this problem will be dealt with in Chapter 11.

Learning a Foreign Language

One of the most useful things that memory aids can help with is the learning of foreign languages. Many people find learning a foreign language both difficult and boring, basically because learning the vocabulary is tedious and time-consuming. But there is no need for learning a language to be like that. A large number of scientific studies have shown how a form of the imagery method can greatly increase the speed, ease and enjoyment of learning a language, at least in the early stages.

The basic method, the key word or Linkword method, involves linking an English word to another English word that sounds like the foreign word you want to learn. For example, the Spanish for *rice* is *arroz*. You remember this by imagining *arrows* landing in your plate of *rice*. Another example is the French word for *tablecloth*, which is *nappe*. You can remember this by imagining yourself having a *nap* on a *tablecloth*.

This method has been used to help people learn a large number of different languages. One of the present authors has published courses that teach English-speakers twelve different languages, as well as teaching German-, French- and Spanish-speakers how to speak English. You can see for yourself now how easy it is to learn vocabulary in any language. We are going to use Welsh as the example because not many English-speakers know Welsh and you cannot judge how effective the method is unless you learn a language you do not already know. In less than half an hour, you will be able to translate up to thirty Welsh words.

A word of warning though. You must spend at least ten seconds thinking about each image, or the words will not stick in your memory. Bear in mind that some languages are easier than others for English speakers to learn. For example, Spanish vocabulary is much easier to learn than Greek, and, of course, there is more to language learning than vocabulary.

NOW TEST YOURSELF

Animals

Think of each image in your mind's eyes for about ten seconds. For example, the Welsh for dog is ci (pronounced key). You should image in your mind's eye a dog carrying a key in its mouth.

	Pronounced
The Welsh for *dog* is *ci*	*(key)*
Imagine a *dog* carrying a *key* in its mouth.	
The Welsh for *cat* is *cath*	(*cath*)
Imagine a cat on top of a *cath*edral.	
The Welsh for *donkey* is *asyn*	(*asin*)
Imagine that hitting a *donkey* is *a sin*.	
The Welsh for *pig* is *mochyn*	(*mochin*)
Imagine *mucking* out a *pig* sty.	
The Welsh for *sheep* is *dafad*	(*davad*)
Imagine *David* in the *Bible* with his sheep.	
The Welsh for *goat* is *gafr*	(*gavr*)
Imagine you *gather goats* as a hobby.	
The Welsh for *animal* is *anifail*	(*aneevile*)
Imagine *an evil animal*.	
The Welsh for *fox* is *cadno*	(*cadno*)
Imagine only a *cad knows* how to kill a *fox*.	
The Welsh for bull is tarw	(*taroo*)
Imagine a *bull* trying to *tire you* out.	

From: © M. M. Gruneberg, Linkword Welsh, Gomer Press, 1995, Black Mountain Records. With permission.

Now turn to the next page.

What is the English for:

Anifail (Aneevile) _____

Gafr (Gavr) _____

Buwch (Bookh) _____

Dafad (Davad) _____

Mochyn (Mochin) _____

Asyn (Asin) _____

Cath (Cath) _____

Ci (Key) _____

Cadno (Cadno) _____

Tarw (Taroo) _____

Turn back for the answers.

Parts of the Body

Think of each image in your mind's eye for about ten seconds.

	Pronounced

The Welsh for *foot* is *troed*   (*troid*)
Imagine you *trod* on your *foot*.

The Welsh for *hand* is *llaw*   (*llow*)
Imagine I *allow* you to bite my *hand*.

The Welsh for *head* is *pen*   (*pen*)
Imagine a *pen* sticking out of your *head*.

The Welsh for *skin* is *croen*   (*croin*)
Imagine *crying* because your *skin* is blue.

The Welsh for *heart* is *calon*   (*calon*)
Imagine your *heart* pumps a *gallon* of blood every minute.

The Welsh for *arm* is *braich*   (*braeech*)
Imagine I *break* your *arm*.

The Welsh for *nose* is *trwyn*   (*trooeen*)
Imagine your *nose* looks as if it has been hit by a *train*.

The Welsh for *finger* is *bys*   (*bees*)
Imagine *bees* stinging your *finger*.

The Welsh for *body* is *corff*   (*korf*)
Imagine your *body* shakes as you *cough*.

The Welsh for *rib* is *asen*   (*asen*)
Imagine Adam gives his *assent* to having his *rib* removed.

Now turn to the next page.

What is the English for:

Bys (bees) _____

Trwyn (trooeen) _____

Braich (braeech) _____

Calon (calon) _____

Croen (croin) _____

Pen (pen) _____

Llaw (llow) _____

Troed (troid) _____

Corff (Korf) _____

Asen (Asen) _____

Turn back for the answers.

Useful Adjectives

Think of each image in your mind's eye for about ten seconds.

	Pronounced
The Welsh for *blue* is *glas* Imagine looking through a *blue glass*.	*(glass)*
The Welsh for *white* is *gwyn* Imagine a pen*guin* has a *white* head. (The feminine form of white is wen.)	*(gwin)*
The Welsh for *yellow* is *melyn* Imagine a *yellow melon*.	*(melin)*
The Welsh for *red* is *coch* Imagine you shoot a *red cock* Robin.	*(coch)*
The Welsh for *pretty* is *pert* Imagine looking at a pretty *pert* girl.	*(pert)*
The Welsh for *old* is *hen* Imagine chasing an *old hen*.	*(hen)*
The Welsh for *ugly* is *hyll* Imagine you look *ugly* standing on a *hill*.	*(hill)*
The Welsh for *quiet* is *tawel* Imagine a *towel* over your head keeps you *quiet*.	*(tahwell)*
The Welsh for *bad* is *drwg* Imagine you take a *bad drug*.	*(droog)*

Now turn to the next page.

What is the English for:

Hyll (hyll) _____

Hen (hen) _____

Pert (pert) _____

Coch (coch) _____

Llwyd (llooeed) _____

Melin (melin) _____

Gwyn (gwin) _____

Glas (glas) _____

Tawel (Tahwell) _____

Drwg (Droog) _____

Turn back for the answers.

As we noted earlier, this approach works for almost any language; courses have been written that help the learning not only of vocabulary but of grammar as well. Studies have shown that the method works with children, the elderly and those good and bad at language learning. However, the method does not work for everyone; people who feel strange making images need to use it for a while so that the strangeness wears off. A number of studies show that most people can pick up a vocabulary of 150–200 words in a day together with a basic grammar, and using this approach can make the acquisition of vocabulary anything from two to three times greater than other methods. It is worth using this method for a while to see if you are comfortable with it.

The Linkword approach to language learning throws up a lot of questions about the teaching of foreign languages. Almost everyone first comes into contact with learning a foreign language at school, where the object is the teach one, or at most, two languages to a reasonably high level in four or five years, in the hope that a few individuals (About 3 per cent of the population of the UK) will progress to a reasonably high level, approaching a working use. Many people, however, do not want to learn a language to this level.

For most of the people living and working in the European Union and indeed business people throughout the world, the real need is often to be able to get by in Berlin on Tuesday, in Paris on Thursday, in Madrid on Friday and in Rome the following Monday. It is totally unrealistic to expect all but a small minority of individuals to master the large range of languages that are frequently needed by the international traveller, yet a great many people would like to learn a language to a level that would enable them to get over the feeling of isolation that comes from not knowing any of the language of the place they are in. It is reassuring to know what you are eating in a restaurant, how to ask for directions in a strange city, and to know how to call a doctor or for help in an emergency, and so on. A few hundred targeted words and a basic grammar, learned quickly with the assistance of memory aids, is exactly what many people want.

It is clear that many people regard a foreign language course as a means to being able to communicate effectively rather than fluently. In other words, being able to cope in a limited number of useful situations is the main goal, and vocabulary is, therefore, all important. You can usually make yourself understood if you have the words, particularly the nouns, but you can't make yourself understood if you know only the grammar. For example, if you are desperate for the toilet and you say 'toilet' in say, Spanish, you will be directed to the toilet. If you say 'I want', you are likely to remain desperate!

As you develop your knowledge of a language, grammar does become important – but never as important as knowing the words. Yet for many people, learning a large number of words quickly is the barrier that prevents them from learning a language at all or even from being interested in trying to learn. One would think that methods such as Linkword, which speed up the process of learning a foreign vocabulary, would be welcomed by teachers, but many language teachers seem to be hostile to the memory aids approach, probably on the grounds that 'if it isn't hurting, it isn't working'. Another reason is that if you already know the language, the use of images to link words looks bizarre, and teachers cannot judge how effective it is.

One objection sometimes raised against all imagery memory aids, including language-learning, is that, because you have to learn the image as well as the words, you have to learn more, so the method cannot be effective! The mistake is to think that the amount of material we have to learn is the main factor that affects memory. It is not.

NOW TEST YOURSELF

Read the following sequence of letters once. Then, without looking at them again, try to recall them.

B R D N   F R C P   G L R

Now look at the same letter sequence only with more letters added.

ABERDEEN FOR CUP GLORY

Cover both sequences and try to remember the letters you were given to start with.

Most people find this extremely easy. *Adding more* information made it *easier* to remember the original letters because it made them more meaningful. It is exactly the same with the use of imagery, including the Linkword method. Using images makes a meaningless association meaningful, and makes it easier, for example, to relate the English word to its foreign equivalent.

What many experiments have shown is that using phrases or images that link two words together, as in the Linkword method, results in the words being far more closely associated together than when they are just repeated together. What is more, once the words are associated together, the image often drops out, so you immediately recall two words together, without thinking of the original image. A large number of studies has found that not only is the imagery approach more effective, it is almost always faster, easier and more enjoyable than other methods, although some readers will, of course, prefer to stick with the methods of name–face association and foreign language study that they are used to.

In summary, this chapter has dealt with two very common memory problems – how to remember people's names, and how to remember vocabulary and grammar when a foreign language is being learned. Both can be improved greatly by using the method of association to link one item to another. For names and faces, the method should only be used for remembering people who are likely to be important to you. The Linkword method has been shown to be effective for learning a foreign language. It too, involves linking two items together using imagery, and language courses that use this principle have been shown to teach a vocabulary of 350–400 words and a basic grammar in ten to twelve hours.

Improving Memory in the Twenty-first Century

Because memory is important to everyone, people have always yearned for ways to improve their memory. For more than 2000 years, specialists have tried to find ways of making memory work better, and as a result, many ingenious methods have been developed to help people with memory tasks, some of which were described in the previous chapters. Recently, however, psychologists, psychiatrists, physicians and other specialists have begun to develop other methods of memory improvement to supplement the classical methods.

Two kinds of method have been researched in the past three decades. First, new methods of mental activity have been developed to enhance memory. One of these is called 'spaced rehearsals'. Rehearsal usually involves repeating information over and over until it sticks in the memory. For example, if a friend's new telephone number is 812357, you may try to commit the number to memory by repeating the number to yourself until you feel you will remember it in the future. Traditional rehearsal was long thought to be one of the best ways to learn something – that is, until spaced rehearsal was developed. Spaced rehearsal involves repeating information once, then waiting a while before repeating it once more, then waiting twice as long before repeating it once again, then waiting twice as long again before repeating the information once more and so on. This pattern of rehearsal has been shown to yield faster and better learning than just repeating the material to yourself over and over again. Next time you have to learn something, just try spaced rehearsal on yourself.

The second method involves improving memory by making sure that a person is in the best possible physical and mental state for remembering. This involves looking at a person's physical condition, not just his or her health but his or her emotional state, his or her attitude and motivation, and whatever stress he or she is under. Research has shown that when someone is in poor shape for any reason, memory performance suffers. On the other hand, it is recognized that people can improve their memory if they acquire better habits of self-care in all aspects of health, emotional circumstances, attitudes, motivation and stress, as well as better social skills, such as conversational skills, as well as using devices that aid memory. This new approach to memory improvement has been called the whole-person or holistic approach. The rest of this chapter describes the whole person approach and how it can be useful to you.

The Case of the Misplaced Keys

Let us illustrate the whole-person approach to memory improvement by considering how to deal with a common everyday memory problem that people find really annoying: remembering *where you put your keys*. Most people who have misplaced their keys retrace their steps by recalling where they have just been, and they also imagine where they typically put the keys. With luck, retracing and imagination will activate the memory to recover the keys.

Although retracing and imagination are good ways of remembering where one has left one's keys, they are not always enough. Sometimes we can be searching for many minutes, even for hours, before we find them. Why aren't retracing and imagination immediately effective?

The main reason people misplace keys is actually not a failure of memory. Factors such as fatigue and stress also often play a part. If you go without sufficient sleep, neglect good eating habits, worry excessively, suffer an emotional upset, or are on a treadmill at work, your mind will lose its focus. The first solution to the case of the misplaced keys then is preventive. If you take steps to reduce stress and to engage in better care of yourself, you will return to your 'best self' and will not misplace the keys in the first place.

Of course, the chance that you will misplace keys will be greatly reduced if you have a regular 'special place' where you always put them. Sometimes, however, people cannot find valuables because they put them in a 'special place' they think that a thief will be unable to find. The problem is that the place is so special that they cannot find it either. Always make sure your special place is one that you will remember.

The second solution to the case of misplaced keys happens when the keys have already been misplaced. If you engage in some last minute self-care – sit down for a minute, take a deep breath and hold it, pick up a magazine for just a minute, and slow down your thoughts – and *then* retrace your steps and imagine your customary spots for putting your keys, you may discover that you will find your keys more quickly.

The Need for Self-care

Few people perform well under pressure, and pressure can cause stress, which, in turn, leads to inadequate sleep, poor nutrition, emotional upsets, and preoccupation with impending difficulties. All these factors interfere with a person's ability to concentrate. People are often so busy that they are unaware of what they are doing, and this lack of awareness prevents them from registering in their memory the precise spot where they put their keys down, the name of the person they met at lunch or the shopping they promised their partners they would do on the way home from work.

The best memory aids in the world will be of little help if a person's psychological processes are not functioning well. If you want to stop forgetting the things that really annoy you, you need to control not only your memory but also your other psychological processes by engaging in good nutrition, rest, and relaxation.

The Case of Remembering What Your Boss Said

Consider how memory techniques and psychological well-being are important to another memory problem. Everyone must recall what their boss says to them at work. If you do not, you may find yourself in your boss's bad books. There are a variety of mental techniques you can use so that you remember your conversations with your boss more accurately. First, reflect on previous conversations with him or her and identify the kinds of thing that your boss typically discusses with you. For example, he or she may expect you to remember the names of the products, old and new, that your company sells. When you have drawn up a list of your boss's favourite topics, study it and you will find that the next time he or she talks with you, the more quickly you will recognize what your boss is talking about and your memory will more easily register what he or she has said.

However, a lack of familiarity with what one's boss says is not usually the whole explanation of why it is difficult to recall your boss's words. Taking part in a conversation demands a great deal of our mind. All you have to do is to tune out just for a second, and you can miss information that is critical to learning and remembering. If the person you are talking with is intimidating, as many bosses are, the challenge of conversation increases. The best mnemonics in the world will be of little help in remembering what your boss says if the stress of dealing with such situations interferes with your ability to pay attention and to use mental tricks.

If you want to remember what is said in any conversation, including those with your boss, you need to prepare for the social stress of a conversation. Stress can be greatly reduced by preparation. First, try to *anticipate* when you will encounter your boss and when the stressful conversations will occur. if you do this, you will not be taken by surprise when the boss arrives and the conversation occurs. Second, *imagine* these conversations beforehand. Prepare yourself by imagining what the boss looks like and how the conversation is likely to go. Think out the answers beforehand, but always be prepared for the unexpected. Act out your part in the conversation and be prepared to admit you do not know the answer to any question if you don't know it. Doing so will make you more comfortable when the real conversation takes place. (See Chapter 17 for a discussion of memory in the workplace.)

The Logic of the New Twenty-first-century Approach

Our memories are affected by our entire psychological system because they are not mechanical devices. Some machines do have memories. A tape recorder, for example, has a 'memory' for what has been recorded. A computer has a 'memory' for what has been keyed into it. But a human's memory is neither a tape recorder nor a computer. Has a tape recorder's or a computer's memory ever failed because it had too little sleep, ate too much, took a sleeping pill or was emotionally upset?

If you can take care of all your physical and psychological processes, you will achieve optimum readiness and your best possible memory performance. Readiness depends on taking care of nine factors that make up our psychological system. Three of the factors are concerned with a person's *physical* states; three are concerned with a person's *emotional* states; and three are concerned with *stimulating* a person's memory. The factors, which combine in the whole-person approach, may be summarized as:

1. Physical states: physical condition, health and chemical state
2. Emotional states: feelings and moods, attitude and motivation
3. Memory stimulation: mental activities, physical environment and social interaction.

In the remainder of this chapter we will look at each of these in turn.

Physical States

Physical Condition

Your ability to perform memory tasks depends on your physical condition, which affects your strength from moment to moment and how your strength is reduced by stress. How much and how well you sleep affects your strength. How much and how well you eat affects your strength, too. Lack of sleep, poor eating habits and a failure to rest reduce your strength, making you less able to perform memory tasks. Eating too large a meal at lunch, or drinking too much alcohol at any time, are examples of poor eating habits that affect memory performance. Thus, improving a poor physical state improves your memory performance.

Health

Illnesses, whether major or minor, interfere with memory because discomfort reduces attention. When our ability to pay attention is lessened, we do not register or remember as well as when we are healthy. Severe physical pain will obviously distract people from attempting to learn and remember. Illnesses typically cause discomfort and reduce energy levels. If they involve a fever, it may affect the brain itself. We will look at health and memory more closely in Chapter 6.

Chemical State

Many common substances can have an adverse effect on memory. Everyday drinks such as coffee, tea and sodas contain stimulants, and tobacco also acts as a stimulant. An excessive use of stimulants makes people more easily distracted and impairs their memory performance. Alcohol and other mind-altering substances interfere with memory, as do medicines that we take for a cold, 'flu or allergies whether they are bought over the counter or with a prescription. A poor chemical state reduces your ability to focus your attention, and any lifestyle changes you can make to produce a better chemical state will improve your memory.

Emotional States

Feelings and Moods

A cheerful, positive state of mind makes it easier for you to learn something than if you are feeling pessimistic or depressed. Everyone has bad days, when everything seems to go wrong and things happen that are upsetting. Your memory does not function well on bad days. A poor emotional state – feelings of anger or depression, for example – reduces your power to focus your attention and, therefore, interferes with your ability to learn and remember. Making an effort to change a bad emotional state into a positive one will improve your memory. Try not to go into an exam, therefore, when there are unresolved quarrels with friends and family. Try to look on the bright side of things, asking yourself 'what is the worst that can happen if things go wrong?' We will look at the effect of your emotional state on memory in more detail in Chapter 7.

Attitude

A positive attitude towards what you need to learn helps greatly in getting the learning done, while a negative attitude can double or triple the amount of time taken to learn. For example, most people dislike having to learn names or French vocabulary or dates or formulae or poems or whatever. Rather than thinking about this in a negative way, remind yourself that almost everyone has this problem. You are definitely not alone. If you make an effort to make a negative attitude less negative, the way your memory performs will improve. If you have a memory task to complete, enjoy it! Feel the satisfaction that gradually comes as you master a subject.

Many people, including many elderly people, have a poor attitude towards memory tasks because they feel they are not going to be successful. Elderly people in particular sometimes think that because they are older, their memory must be bad, and consequently, they don't even try to remember as much as they could. Then when they don't remember, they conclude it was because of their age, when in fact it was because they did not try enough. A poor attitude leads to a self-fulfilling prophecy.

Motivation

Rewards and punishments affect memory in the same way that they affect other types of behaviour. People typically learn and remember the names of their bosses faster than the names of their colleagues. It is not that people are sycophantic, it is simply that the *positive incentives* for learning and the negative incentives for forgetting are higher with a superior's name than with the names of co-workers. A negative motivational state reduces your ability to pay attention while you are, say, being introduced to a colleague. However, making a bad motivational state better can improve your memory performance.

If you are interested in a topic, you will find it far easier to remember new information about it. Research has shown, for example, that people who are interested in football or chess remember far more about football scores and chess positions that people who are not interested. A healthy interest in a topic can make a person remember a lot of information without even trying.

Memory Stimulation

Mental Activities

Our minds constantly take in new information. Some of this information is registered so strongly that it become permanent immediately. For example, people remember very well personally important events such as when President Kennedy was shot or when they experienced their first kiss. However, the amount of detail registered is small unless we pay attention to the content of our conscious thoughts. The more we think about something, the more meaningful it becomes, and therefore more of it will be registered permanently.

Physical Environment

A note will often remind us to do something, and some commercial memory aids also help our memory greatly. Timers and alarm clocks, for instance, remind us to do things generally more accurately than the biological clock inside us. Some appliances relieve us of the burden of remembering entirely – video recorders, for example, switch themselves on and off when left unattended. If you can arrange for the environment to provide you with enough clues, you *will* have a better chance of remembering. Chapter 9 reviews a wide range of memory devices which you may find useful.

Social interaction

When we are with other people, our minds are usually challenged to learn and remember much more than when we are alone. Interacting with people is distracting, making it hard to concentrate, but it does make your memory work for you. Failure at many memory tasks can hurt your relationships with other people. If you forget someone's name your relationship with that person my be at risk. An awareness of social factors and social skills can substantially improve your learning and remembering while you are with other people. Chapter 8 will review aspects of social interaction that can increase the chances of memory success.

In summary, recent scientific investigations of memory have made it clear that memory performance is due not only to a person's memory aptitude but also to the entire psychological system. Many memory failures are due to a deterioration in physical states or emotional states. Make sure your physical state is a good one for memory: make sure that you are getting enough good things to eat, enough sleep, enough rest, and enough exercise. Check whether life events have piled up on you. If necessary, share your emotional problems with a friend or someone else you trust. Examine your health, especially your use of chemicals. Make sure you are not using to excess substances or medicines that are making you jittery or dull, sleepy or depressed.

Health and Memory

When we feel ill or have aches and pains, we cannot expect ourselves to be as sharp as usual. There is evidence that people sometimes fail at memory tasks because they do not feel well or because they are tired. There is also evidence that if you have a low-grade fever or a chill or if you are taking certain medicines, your memory can be badly affected. An awareness and understanding of how ill health affects your memory can prepare you to recognize when your health is affecting your memory.

When you are in poor health, your memory system is less efficient for several reasons. First, attention, which is so essential to memory performance, is reduced. If you do not pay attention to what is happening then, obviously, ideas and images are not likely to be registered strongly in your memory. Second, poor health makes remembering more difficult because you often fail to notice clues that can help you to remember and because the energy needed to search your memory is just not there. To restore the memory system to its proper level, it is necessary to return to good health.

Good health is especially important to the performance of memory tasks in which you unconsciously learn and remember while doing other things. Of course, the healthier you are, the more you are likely to perform at your best on all memory tasks. If you can anticipate a day on which you will want to be at your intellectual best – for an important meeting or an exam for instance – take care of your physical and emotional state a few days before that date. Let us consider in more detail those aspects of your health that you need to attend to.

Physical Condition

Any factor that saps your strength will undermine your memory. Any factor that causes you pain will distract you and also undermine your memory. It is therefore important to your memory to be physically fit, healthy, well rested and relaxed.

Physical Fitness
Exercise helps you maintain your strength and keeps your heart and arteries in good condition. Strength and good circulation help you stand up to a hard day and help your memory to function when others are too tired to try. Exercise can also help relieve you of the 'blues' and stress.

Depression and stress impair memory. If you are depressed or stressed, you are much less likely to pay attention to what is going on around you. You are also much less likely to 'try' to remember what is happening and what you have already stored in your memory. Exercise improves memory when a person is depressed or stressed, and it also improves sleep, and better sleep leads to better mental functioning. Of course, exercise on its own cannot solve deep-rooted problems that make a person depressed or stressed, but it can help if the problems are the everyday hassles that get to everyone from time to time.

Peak Times.
It is important to recognize that our mental strength varies across the day, going up and down. Everyone has a personal peak time, and most people find that it comes somewhere between the late morning and mid-afternoon. After lunch, we get drowsy for a little while and then recover. Later in the day we gradually wear down again. Our

ability to pay attention increases and decreases with these variations in mental strength; we learn and remember best at our 'peak times'.

A change in your daily or weekly routine means you have to readjust. We notice this particularly if we have to travel across time zones, especially when we end up with jet lag. Such travel often seriously disrupts memory. When you get jet lag, you might find it hard to remember directions on how to get to your hotel or, once in the hotel, to remember the number of your room. When you travel across time zones, you should allow extra time to recover before taking on tasks that rely on judgement and memory.

Your sleep patterns also affect when you feel mentally strongest and most energetic. Your memory works best at these peak times. If you go to bed early and get up early, you probably learn more readily at the beginning of the day. If you go to bed late and get up late, you are probably sharper later in the day. If you work a night shift or at weekends, your peak times are probably different from those of people who work from nine to five, Monday to Friday.

Your peak time will also depend on how much sleep you have recently been getting. A good night's sleep will make you strong and alert for memory tasks. A late night studying for work or school can result in tiredness the next day, and this can make you struggle to remember answers that you would normally have no difficulty in remembering.

Because we are all different, it is important that you work out your own peak times for yourself. It does not matter to you if 80 per cent of people peak in the afternoon, if you peak in the morning. Try getting up early in the morning, say about 6am, to see if the early morning is a good period for you to work in – at least it is usually quiet. Remember, too, that you can make use of your non-peak times to carry out less demanding mental or physical work. Once you are sure when your peak times occur, take advantage of them and perform memory tasks when your reserves are at their highest. If you have an important meeting coming up, try to schedule it during your peak time.

Nutrition

Many nutritionists have suggested that vitamins help memory, but just about every nutritionist also advises that a normal, healthy diet supplies enough vitamins to guard against memory-related deficiencies. Generally, protein-rich foods help memory: beef, pork, kidneys, liver, fish, shellfish, milk, eggs, cheese and vegetables, including kelp and onions.

Some supplements, called 'memory boosters' because they combine the various memory nutrients in one pill, are available. Such supplements are normally safe to take, although the use of megadoses of some vitamins or minerals is not recommended. Always read the label on the container. In our judgement, these supplements will not improve the memory performance of people who eat a normal, well-balanced diet, but may well help some people suffering from a vitamin deficiency, such as children who are 'addicted' to junk food. We do not recommend that you take vitamins as a way to improve your memory power unless it is impossible to change your diet to include vitamin-rich foods.

However, there is one substance that has recently been discovered to have beneficial effects on memory – glucose, the natural form of sugar that comes in fruits and can be obtained from some pharmacies or health food stores. Glucose helps your memory especially when your glucose level is low. It has been shown that elderly people who have taken glucose about twenty minutes before studying something perform better than average.

Whatever your typical diet, do not eat to excess before you have to perform important memory tasks. Large quantities of food make people drowsy and unable to learn and remember, and being overweight leads to a loss of fitness as well as some major illnesses.

Eyesight and Hearing Difficulties

Some memory failures are actually not due to poor memory as such but due to sensory problems. Poor eyesight or poor hearing often prevents a person from being aware of things, and obviously, if you do not see an event or hear a conversation in the first place, you cannot register it in your memory. If others around you do not know you have poor eyesight or hearing problems, they will think that you were simply not paying attention to what they saw or heard. Later, when you cannot remember what was observed, other people will think you have a bad memory. Unfortunately, when you explain that you were not able to see or hear properly, you colleagues will not believe you. Instead, they will see you as making excuses for your memory failure.

If you really think that one of your senses is failing, get yourself examined by a physician. You may find out that all you need is a loudness amplifier for your telephone or a magnifying glass for reading fine print. if it turns out that you need reading glasses or a hearing aid, you will be glad when you perform far better at memory tasks that others ask of you.

If you or your child are experiencing seeing or hearing problems, tell other people about these beforehand. If others are forewarned, they will be more considerate about the way they communicate with you. They will also be less likely to accuse you of memory failure for things you never perceived in the first place. The possibility that poor eyesight and poor hearing are affecting children at school must also be borne in mind. If your child is doing badly at school, it is vitally important he or she has a full physical examination, including eyesight and hearing tests.

Illness

Illness lessens our physical and mental strength and usually causes us to feel discomfort and pain. Some illnesses interfere with our thought processes, and at the extreme, serious illnesses can sometimes make a person delirious.

Although people recognize that serious illness can interfere with mental ability, many people act as if minor illnesses have no effect on memory. Unfortunately, there is plenty of evidence to suggest that even minor illnesses disturbs memory and thought processes.

Think about it. Have you ever had to give a speech from memory when you had a bad cold? The chances are that you were slow in remembering what you intended to say. Have you ever been at work when you have had an upset stomach? This will have essentially the same effect as having a bad cold. Even being pregnant can produce temporary memory problems. The table below shows how some fairly common illnesses can interfere with memory.

Examples of Common Illnesses that Impair Memory

Arthritis	Arthritis causes a great deal of pain that interferes with the concentration necessary for learning and remembering.
Boils	Boils are painful and, because they are ugly, they make people unhappy, causing them to perform memory tasks poorly.
Heart disease	People who have had a heart attack often lose some short-term memory ability.
Influenza	While a person is suffering from 'flu, he or she becomes more easily confused and disorientated, especially if he or she has a high fever.
Malaria	While a person has malaria, he or she is confused and disorientated. After the illness, flashbacks may occur, again producing confusion and interfering with memory.

There are several reasons why mental tasks, including memory tasks, become more difficult when we are ill. Almost all illnesses cause some discomfort and pain, and experiencing discomfort and pain makes it hard to pay attention. When our ability to pay attention is lessened, we do not register information and we miss clues that would help us to remember. Consequently, people who fall ill frequently have significantly more memory problems than people who stay in good health.

If you have an event coming up that is going to challenge your memory – giving a speech, taking an exam, or attending an interview, for example – and you are ill, try to postpone it. Do not go if at all possible. If you do, you will not be at your best. If it is impossible to postpone the event, get a lot of rest, over-prepare and avoid doing work beforehand.

Some illnesses impair memory so severely that they're known as 'memory illnesses'. Alzheimer's disease, which is probably the most widely known of these conditions, has a progressive and devastating effect on the memory abilities of those who suffer from it. Korsakoff's syndrome is another illness that affects memory. Caused by excessive alcoholic consumption over a prolonged period, the syndrome involves a severe loss of the ability to register new memories.

A major stroke, which sends a blood clot to the brain, seriously disrupts memory, often permanently, while mini-strokes, which send many tiny clots to the brain, can also impair memory, but not usually permanently. Very low blood pressure, which is a life-threatening condition, also impairs memory because it lessens your ability to pay attention. If you believe that you have developed one of these serious illnesses, you should consult a physician. (The effects of brain damage on memory are discussed in more detail in Chapter 15.)

Treatment

Medicines
Every kind of medicine has side-effects, some of which interfere with memory performance. Generally, any medicine that makes you sleepy will impair memory. Most antihistamines and cold medicines, for example, have this effect, as do most tranquillizers, some anti-depressants and, of course, sleeping pills, which will affect you even the next day, after a good night's rest. Any medicine that makes you jumpy, such as stimulants and many diet pills, can also affect memory.

If you are taking medication that has been prescribed for some ailment, ask your doctor if it has side-effects that will interfere with memory and if there is an alternative available that might not affect memory or might, at least, not have such a serious effect on it. This is particularly important in the case of depression, which is a condition that can seriously damage memory. Some anti-depressant medicines help the depression, but make memory worse, while other anti-depressant medicines appear not to damage memory. If you are in any doubt, discuss this with your doctor. Below are a list of medications that have been found in some cases to impair memory and thinking.

Drugs that can Impair Memory and Cognition

AMPHETAMINES, ANALGESICS, ANTIAXIOLYTICS, ANTIBIOTICS, ANTI-DEPRESSANTS, ANTI-DIABETICS, ANTI-HISTAMINES, ANTI-EMETICS, ANTIHYPERTENSIVES, ANTIPSYCHOTICS, BARBITURATES, DIGITALIS, GLAUCOMA EYE DROPS, LITHIUM, SEDATIVES, TRANQUILLIZERS

In summary, optimize your memory by maintaining good physical condition. Eat a well-balanced diet and avoid over-eating before you are going to perform important memory tasks. Get enough sleep regularly so that you are strong and alert enough to register and remember information. Take account of your peak times. Schedule memory tasks for times when you are mentally strongest and most attentive. Stay in shape. Recognize that minor illness can make you less sharp. Discomfort distracts, so remember that learning and memory require physical and mental strength. Understand the side-effects of your medication, and seek out memory-friendly medicine when possible. Avoid substances such as stimulants that can impair your ability to pay attention.

7
Emotional States

Everyone gets upset from time to time, but when people find that they have to perform memory tasks while they are upset, the consequence is usually that they perform less well than usual. The cause of the emotional upset can range from hearing disturbing or unpleasant news about a relative or friend to a major personal crisis. When a series of events disturbs us in some way, we say we are under stress, and if the events are pleasing, if they are more than we can handle, they can also be stressful.

Disturbing events, whether they happen singly or as a series of events, will have negative effects on our memory and thinking. Emotional upset leads people to become confused, to have difficulty in paying attention and to become less able to learn and remember.

Confusion

When someone is confused, his or her level of attention decreases. At such times, anything you can do to slow down your world, even a little bit, will help your concentration and general memory skills.

A hectic and harried lifestyle leaves otherwise fit people disorientated. If you sense occasionally that you are confused or at least not concentrating, try to alter your daily routine to improve your concentration. Don't slow it down too much, however. A predictable and routine lifestyle may give you the feeling that you are in a rut, and this, too, can lessen your ability to concentrate.

You also have to beware of tasks that you do very well. It is quite possible that you are so adept at a task that you are relaxed and can do several other things at the same time. Proficiency is admirable and rewarding, of course, but sometimes it backfires. Research shows that when you have a great deal of experience at a task, your performance sometimes becomes so automatic that you stop paying full attention to it. Driving is an excellent example of this. At some points during a journey, you are totally aware of every turn you make; at other times you suddenly realize that your mind has been elsewhere for many miles.

Moods

Negative moods – feeling down, angry or aggressive, for example – can impair memory performance. A slightly negative mood, such as being irritated about something that went wrong at work, may make you preoccupied, and at such a time you will not attend as well as you should to the world about you. An intensely negative mood, such as the anger generated by an argument with someone you care about, is even more draining. Anger or rage is likely to energize you too much and distract you from performing memory tasks well.

Real depression, as distinct from feeling 'down', is very hard on memory. It lowers your level of attention and reduces your capacity to focus attention. Severe depression weakens memory so much that some doctors regard complaints about memory failure as a symptom of depression. When depression is treated, typically with anti-depressant drugs and/or psychotherapy, memory powers soon return, provided the drug used does not itself have adverse effects on memory (see Chapter 6). Always check with your doctor, and tell him or her you have read that some anti-depressant drugs affect memory. If he or she does not give a satisfactory answer, check with the pharmacist.

Stress

Stress can seriously interfere with memory. People who suffer a lot of stress report many memory failures, and it is known that people who work in high-stress jobs have more memory failures than those who work in jobs with an average amount of stress.

Some stress is better than none at all, however, and although too much anxiety before a test will distract you and hamper your recall, the absence of any anxiety may mean you are not taking the test seriously enough and are not putting your maximum effort into doing well. A little anxiety will keep you alert and ready to tackle memory tasks as they arise. The trick is to manage your stress level so that it does not get too low or too high.

One of the best ways to reduce stress is by relaxing. How to relax is a personal matter – some people listen to classical music, while others find rock and roll relaxing. Some people relax by doing some form of exercise, while others prefer to sit still, read or watch television. Whichever method suits you, relaxation will improve your mood and increase your potential to concentrate, which, in turn, improves memory performance.

Today many different kinds of relaxation methods are available commercially. One method, called 'positive imaging' or 'creative visualization', involves learning how to create comforting imagery. A second method involves experiencing 'sensory deprivation', when someone is put in a container that keeps his or her seeing, hearing and feeling to a minimum. The container, the Lily Tank, blocks out all light and sound, and restricts movement. A third method, alpha wave control, involves learning how to control brain waves to put yourself into a relaxing state of mind. A fourth method, biofeedback, involves learning how to control your blood pressure and pulse rate so that you can bring them into the right range for relaxation.

Yet another system, neurolinguistic programming, involves learning to control what one says to oneself, while a sixth method is to play tapes or CDs of soothing music or peaceful sounds, such as that of the ocean lapping on the shore. Properly used, all of these systems can reduce stress and facilitate your memory performance, at least in the short term.

Negative Emotions

If you need to register in your memory something that is very upsetting, it is usually easier to remember the event or information later. Strongly negative events are, in fact, so easy to register that sometimes we cannot forget them no matter how hard we try. On the other hand, if you need to register something that is only mildly upsetting, it is often difficult to recall it later. The negative emotion may suppress the memory, and your mind may block it out so you don't have to face it. Suppression of negative feelings is common. Many people miss appointments with their doctor or dentist, for instance, because the experience of going to the doctor reminds them of prior sickness and pain.

Suppression protects us from dwelling on unpleasant matters. Nevertheless, if you have to learn and remember something unpleasant, you need to protect the memory against suppression. Try to persuade yourself to view the negative information positively, although obviously, this may not always be possible or appropriate.

Traumatic Emotions

Although it is often hard to forget very upsetting memories, humans are able to banish certain traumatic experiences from their memories. It seems to be that we are so shocked that we don't remember the memory at all. According to Sigmund Freud, these memories are so threatening that we unconsciously struggle to repress them.

While *suppressed* memories can be remembered with effort and sufficient cues, *repressed* memories cannot be remembered by conventional mental strategies, such as increasing the number of cues present. Repression removes any awareness of the information from our conscious memory. Many psychologists believe that we all repress some of our memories to a degree, and some people repress so many memories that it becomes a serious problem. They are said to be out of touch with reality.

Freud believed that repressed memories are remembered only after recalling many related memories (a process Freud called 'psychoanalysis'), which helps to explain why the event was so upsetting in the first place. If you suspect that you may have repressed some important memories and it is interfering with your happiness, consult a clinical psychologist or psychiatrist about the problem. The recovery of repressed memories is something we cannot expect to do on our own.

Sometimes, instead of suppressing or repressing a memory, we *distort* a part of it. For instance, you may have a terrible job interview or an unfriendly exchange with someone you considered a friend. Afterwards, you may try to convince yourself that things didn't go as badly as they really did. Sometimes we distort a memory deliberately because the fantasy helps us accept what happened. Once a memory is distorted, the distortion is difficult to detect because it protects our self-image. We want the events of our lives to be consistent with our self-image and goals.

Motivation and Emotions

Give a person enough money to learn something, and there is a very good chance he or she will succeed. The financial incentive is the motivation that increases the person's attention and makes him or her try harder when using mental strategies. Motivation of any kind boosts a person's mood and provides a reason to gain control over their emotions. Give a person money to remember something, and usually he or she will recall more, especially if he or she wasn't trying before. However, all the money in the world will not get a person to recall what cannot be accessed in their memory when he or she truly tries to remember.

If you are feeling 'down' but you have to attend a dull lecture or business meeting that you sense may be important to you in the future, take extra care to get yourself mentally 'up' for the occasion. Don't give in to your temptation to scoff at the material or to do other work. Take careful notes. Try to think of ways you could make the material more useful to you. Convince yourself that while the experience may be unpleasant, some greater good will come of it. Identify information that is uninteresting but important for you to know, and take extra steps to make sure that you will remember it.

You must convince yourself that although the material is boring, you simply have to learn it. However, if you can't convince yourself, then reward yourself for sitting through it and paying attention. Say to yourself: 'If I can only make it through this next hour, I'll give myself £50 or $100 – or whatever it takes.' If you can't find an adequate reward – that is, if no reward is big enough – try this, if you dare. Brag to your associates or colleagues that you have a photographic memory for lectures. They will, we promise, check your recall afterwards and humiliate you if your memory isn't as good as you claimed.

There is a lot to know about your emotional states and memory. Below is a list of the states that you need to attend to.

Motivational State

INCENTIVES TO LEARN OR REMEMBER

PERSONAL GOALS

UNREWARDED INFORMATION

UNINTERESTING INFORMATION

UNPLEASANT INFORMATION

PERSONALLY UPSETTING INFORMATION

EGO-THREATENING INFORMATION

UNCONSCIOUS MOTIVES

There are several ways in which you can take account of your emotional state and improve your memory performance. Avoid both a hectic lifestyle and a monotonous lifestyle: too little activity lessens your capacity to pay attention, just as too much activity does. Keep stress within a manageable range, and give extra rehearsal to any slightly negative memories that you cannot afford to forget.

Relax regularly or, if you cannot manage that, at least try to relax before you know your memory will be challenged. Go for a walk or do some yoga or some other kind of exercise that you enjoy. Stay in brightly lit surroundings as darkness can sometimes be depressing. We learn and remember best when we are in a neutral or slightly 'up-beat' mood.

When you are feeling anxious, take a deep breath and hold it. Relax and allow yourself to think about whatever it is that is making you anxious. Make sure that you think positively but gradually. If you catch yourself thinking negatively, rephrase your thoughts to be positive and repeat these positive thoughts. Alternatively, engage in daydreaming; imagine places that you have enjoyed visiting. If you are going through a bad period, talk through your problems with someone you can trust. Having a better outlook will help your memory.

Many memory tasks sneak up on you when you are least well prepared. For example, on the spur of the moment, a friend brings an important guest over to meet you and you have to try to get to know the person, even though you don't feel up to it. The only way to get your memory to cope successfully with the tasks that you didn't anticipate is to try to improve your emotional state. This is because memory aids of the kind we discussed in Chapters 1 and 2 often involve preparation beforehand.

Generally, good preparation requires that you check your motivation for tasks before they confront you. Motivation will increase your attention and make you try harder when you are using mental strategies. On the next page is a list of those aspects of motivation that you should be aware of and aim to have under your control.

Emotional State

ANXIETY IN GENERAL LEVEL *AND* REGARDING
     MEMORY PERFORMANCE

AROUSAL

CONFUSION AND DISTRACTION

EMOTIONAL EXTREMES: ELATION – DEPRESSION

EMOTIONAL TRAUMA – REPRESSION

MOOD

PREOCCUPATION AND WORRY

STRESS

Don't give in to a temptation to be negative about work you have to do. Convince yourself that while an experience may be uninteresting, some greater good will come of it. Identify information that is uninteresting but important for you to know, and take extra steps to make sure that you will remember it. If you allow yourself to be bored by information you need to learn, you will have to work five times harder to learn it.

Social Skills

Whenever we are with other people we have to use our memory a lot: we must recall their names and remember what they do; we must make and meet appointments; we must return favours and do tasks that others depend on us to do; and we must recall information and remember past events. While we use our memory in these ways, we must also smile and frown, shift our gaze from one person to another, walk and gesture.

Who and what we remember affects how others judge and treat us. If you remember what you are supposed to, you will usually be rewarded with appreciation, affection and even love. Your friends and associates will think that you are considerate and sensitive and that you care about them. If, for example, you send a card and a present to your partner on your wedding anniversary, you will at least be rewarded with an affectionate kiss. If, on the other hand, you forget something important, you will be punished in some way. Your family, friends and acquaintances will think that you don't care about them, or that you have become self-centred. They may even wonder about your intelligence or doubt your emotional stability.

Because your relationships with others can be seriously affected by your performance in social memory tasks, carrying out these tasks successfully is very important. If you want others to respect your memory powers, you must remember those things that others value.

Unfortunately, your memory is more likely to fail when you are with others than when you are alone. When you are with others, your mind is doubly burdened. You not only have to recall what you know but you must respond to what others say and remember. Thus, extra steps must be taken to prepare your memory to perform well in social situations. Several factors make memory less dependable when you are in social situations, and we will discuss the five most important of these:

1. We are *expected* to learn and remember certain information about others.
2. We need the skills for directing the *flow of conversation* so that we have enough time to learn and remember before the conversation passes on.
3. People sometimes give us *bad data*, either lies or just incorrect information, and we make the mistake of believing them.
4. We do not realize that we should resist *social pressures* to distrust our memory.
5. We do not know how to *persuade* others that our memory is as accurate as we claim.

You can do things to counteract these five factors and make your memory perform better. Next you will learn about how you can control these factors.

Expectations

People we know well, as well as those we know less well, expect us to meet appointments with them or do certain tasks that affect them. When it comes to people we regard as friends, we should also know what they know. We should know, say, which political candidates they favour. We should remember to do tasks for them in a reasonable interval if we have promised to do something. A friend will question the sincerity of your friendship simply because you do not realize what this person expects you to remember.

Many of the expectations others have of us are subtle and never stated. For example, we kiss some friends but not others. We hug some relatives but not others. We shake hands with some people and not others. If you kiss the wrong person or you do not kiss someone who expects it, you will get yourself in trouble. Hug the wrong person or do not hug the right person, and again you will be in trouble. Fail to shake hands with some business associates, and they will be insulted.

Some social expectations are obvious – remembering and saying someone's name, for example – and we can focus on and learn the obvious expectations. We can make notes on them and consult them later. Some people even keep notebooks with information about their friends and associates.

Some expectations are unstated. Sometimes a loved one, a friend or an acquaintance expects us to know something although he or she has never actually said so. For example, people may expect us to remember their accomplishments, and our partners expect birthdays and holidays to be remembered with gifts.

The main way to detect the expectations of a loved one, friend, or acquaintance is through paying careful attention to feedback. For example, sometimes friends tells you about something they did of which they were clearly proud. Make an effort to memorize this achievement and to mention it on a later occasion. They will smile and may even compliment you on your memory.

Sometimes people expect you to remember something because you have a *reputation* for having a good memory. Among the people you have known for a while, you may have gained a reputation for how well you succeed – or fail – at memory tasks. Your memory reputation is, of course, part truth and part fiction, based on your past memory performance and what others have said to each other about your memory. Regardless of the accuracy of your reputation, some people will be inclined to believe what others say about your memory. If someone believes you are good at remembering something, you had better remember it or they will be offended or angry.

Most people would prefer to have a reputation for having a good memory, but, perhaps surprisingly, such a reputation has its drawbacks. You are likely to have extra responsibilities. If you are known for 'always remembering details', people may expect you to remember more information than they would ask of others. Similarly, a reputation for having a poor memory can have advantages. People will be reluctant to burden you with memory tasks, giving you extra time to pursue your own interests.

It is a sad fact, but someone may have expectations of your memory that are based on prejudice. People can, of course, be prejudiced for many reasons: they may dislike a person because of age, sex, nationality, race, occupation and/or religion. This prejudice will affect the way they view a person's memory. When age is considered, for example, it is true that an older person's memory may not be as good as that of someone who is younger, but it is not automatically true, because many older people have excellent memories. Another example of how prejudice can influence a person's perception of someone's memory has to do with the person's sex. Some people think that men are good at remembering phone numbers and women are good at remembering names; this is true as often as it is untrue. What is said to be true about a group is never true about all the members of that group.

Ironically, prejudicial attitudes often influence one's expectations of oneself. For example, many elderly people believe that their memory ability is poor, when, in fact, it is quite normal. Many people think they are bad at remembering groceries, while others think that they are bad at remembering directions, even though their skills in this area are frequently pretty good.

Another source of expectations is a 'memory pact', to which we have agreed. People who are married or who live together often share responsibilities for their home, including memory tasks. For example, one person agrees to perform one memory task and the partner agrees to do another: 'you remember to pick up the milk, and I'll remember to take things to the dry cleaners.' A pact like this usually makes expectations clear. Consequently, when you fail to remember to do what you agreed to, you will get a lot of grief from your partner.

Conversational Skills

As we have already noted, your memory is more likely to fail when you are with other people than when you are alone. This happens because conversations are often distracting, making it hard to use your memory effectively. Memory fails especially if the flow of conversation is too fast, and in particular if it shifts from one person to another.

Keeping track of the topics covered in conversation is hard; remembering the points made is harder; and remembering to make all the points you would like to make is harder still. Many conversations require us to recall past events and information, and we are sometimes put on the spot when someone asks us to remember something that they expect us to know. In order to pick up and retain what others say, or to have enough time to remember something, it is helpful to acquire certain conversational skills, which can help you to avoid being seen as ignorant of something that others feel you should know.

One such skill involves altering the flow of conversation so that you have enough time to remember things that are not easily remembered. If you think you can recall something if you have enough time, do things to make yourself that time. For example, suppose you are asked a question, but the answer does not come immediately to mind. To buy the time you need, try one or more of the following ploys. Shift the topic of conversation. Ask someone else what they think the answer is. Seize the floor and give a short discourse on a related topic until the information you are trying to remember finally comes to you. Of course, if you know you will not remember, regardless of how much time you have, you may want to admit your failure straightaway. People are usually more ready to forgive memory failures if we are honest about them. On the other hand, some memory failures, such as the failure to remember the name of someone you should know, are usually best not admitted!

Bad Data

Sometimes a person unintentionally remembers something incorrectly, and sometimes people lie. If other people are not honest with you about what they recall, or if they recall incorrectly, you receive incorrect or distorted information. In order for you to store in your memory the most accurate information possible, it is important that you learn how to detect whether what others say is accurate or not.

People may lie about their opinion of your memory. They may say that your memory is bad just to insult you; alternatively, they may say your memory is good just to flatter you. If someone says something good or something bad about your memory, consider whether they are lying or telling the truth. If you do not realize someone is lying and you believe you have been insulted, you will lose confidence in your memory. If you believe false praise, you will become overconfident about your memory.

Social Pressure

People sometimes assert confidently that they do not believe what we recall, and their doubt may make us doubt ourselves. For example, if you are talking to your friends about an occasion when you have had a good time, your experience of the event may be different and you may recall events differently from several of your friends. They may say your memory is bad, and this may make you feel you should revise your memory so that it is consistent with their version. This doubt can arise even when you are initially sure of your recollection, even if your memory is actually right. People find it especially stressful to be the 'odd one out' among well-respected friends or with a figure who is in authority. Nevertheless, it is a shame if you allow yourself to be persuaded that your memory is wrong when it is really correct.

It is not possible to suggest an easy way to insulate your memory from group pressures. Bear in mind, however, that when someone else says your memory is wrong, it may be right and their memory may be at fault. Because you could be right, guard against revising your memory just because someone else says you are wrong. If another person attacks your recall, try to check for corroborating evidence when you have a chance.

If someone tells you that your recall of something is wrong and you would have sworn you were right, don't give in. Re-examine the facts as you recall them. If you decide you are wrong, admit it. But if the facts seem right to you, hold your ground. Don't let someone else's views influence your impression of yourself and lead you to recall incorrectly.

Persuasion skills

Even if you have successfully recalled something, you may still fail to *communicate* it in a way that makes others believe you. People will be more inclined to believe you if you follow certain rules when you are telling them what you recall. These rules are:

1. Make sure that all parts of your recollection tie in with each other. Contradictions between facts you recall indicate that the memory underlying your report is distorted.
2. Choose your words carefully. Even if you are right, your words can mislead others. If you use the wrong term to describe something, others will distrust the accuracy of your memory.
3. Make your recall as complete as possible. When we are in a hurry or under stress, we omit details or mis-state points. An omission can get us into trouble. Support your information with sources that are independent of yourself. Your recall will be more readily accepted if you have an independent outside source, such as newspapers, books or memos.

4. Express your views in a convincing manner, using an appropriate amount of confidence when you speak. What you say about your confidence in the recall is critical. Overstatement or understatement in your recall will make you seem dishonest. You must convey the appropriate degree of certainty with the right words. If your memory is poor, you may say that you 'suspect' or 'believe'. If your memory is very good, say you 'know', 'guarantee' or even 'swear' that something you recall is true.

5. Make sure that your relationship is good with the people you want to believe you. When it is important that someone else believes what you recall, be friendly. If the person listening to you is on good terms with you, this person will be more likely to accept your recall as valid. Your relationship with other people extends to the way you treat the recall of others.

6. Be polite. There is an unwritten code of memory etiquette: if you have criticized someone else's memory, it will usually come back to haunt you. For example, if someone forgets items just mentioned in a discussion and you point this out, you will appear rude. If you must correct someone's recall, do so politely, and it is wise to ignore unimportant memory errors, especially if the person is a loved one. People will be inclined to expect more or less of your memory according to how you get on with them.

7. Use another person as a memory aid only if it is absolutely necessary. Sometimes we do not feel like making an effort at a memory task that arises in conversation. Instead, we may try to use someone else to help, perhaps asking him or her to answer a question that we could have answered if we really tried. Or we ask him or her to register and retain some information and to tell us about it later. Or we may ask him or her to remind us later when we are supposed to do something.

Although it is often easier to ask someone in a meeting with us to take notes about what is being said, you should be careful about relying on someone else to do your learning for you. If he or she is angry with you, he or she may refuse to provide the facts you had asked him or her to remember or remind you of. In addition, the person may honestly forget. Use another person as a memory aid rarely. If you do, do so with a full appreciation that the other person may let you down or expect you to pay him or her back.

In summary, social situations require us to perform many memory tasks. This chapter has discussed a variety of things that you can do to make your memory perform better in social contexts: recognizing the important memory tasks that others expect you to perform; directing the flow of conversation so that you have enough time to learn and remember; detecting and ignoring bad data; resisting social pressures to distrust your memory; and expressing yourself in ways that persuade others that your memory is as accurate as you claim.

You now know more about how you can use your memory more effectively when you are with others. This knowledge will be useful to you in many situations, at work and at home.

Memory
Devices

What we see and hear affects memory powerfully. Seeing people in person – in the flesh – evokes far more memories than just thinking about them. Because objects and sounds have such a big impact on memory, people have devised ways to make use of natural objects to stimulate their memories.

Memory aids work primarily because physical objects and events have a powerful effect on our minds. Indeed, objects and events capture our attention better than most ideas do. Because they may aid memory so well, many 'external aids' have been developed, both by ordinary citizens and by large companies, and because external aids can help your memory so much, a good knowledge of them is essential if we are to be able to treat memory problems. This chapter reviews how you may use external memory aids to improve your memory performance and, in some cases, even relieve you of the burden of having to perform some memory tasks altogether.

There are at least seven kinds of external memory device. The most common is the memory helper, which can be used to improve memory performance. A memory robot can carry out a memory task – a calculator, for example, will perform division and multiplication that otherwise must be done mentally. A memory corrector can remember something you have forgotten or work out something that has stumped you. A teaching machine presents material to be learned in the best way – there are, for example, software programs that help people learn foreign languages. A memory measurer tests a person's memory – one device, for example, asks people to rate the functioning of their memory from time to time. Memory art presents information that a person needs to study or that will cue the person to remember. Memory awakeners are intended to help people remember their past and reminisce, while superstitious memory aids involve objects that an individual had with him or her when his or her memory performed exceptionally well – students, for example, often take a 'lucky pen' with them when they have to take an exam.

The following list is of different kinds of external memory aid. The remainder of this chapter provides several examples of each kind of aid and describes how they may be used to improve your memory performance. After the different kinds of aids are explained, we will indicate several situations in everyday life in which external aids are useful.

Kinds of External Memory Aid

MEMORY HELPER	MEMORY MEASURER
MEMORY ROBOT	MEMORY ART
MEMORY CORRECTOR	MEMORY AWAKENERS
MEMORY TRAINERS	SUPERSTITIOUS MEMORY AIDS

Memory Helper

Memory helpers are devices that make it more likely that a person will learn and remember, but they cannot guarantee that this will happen. They range from timers that can be set to remind you to do something when a bell or buzzer sounds to more complicated devices. Helpers are the largest group of such memory aids and the following pages describe some of the major types.

Back-up records

When a secretary takes dictation or a court stenographer records a trial, they do so because an unaided memory often fails. A back-up record of your intentions is very helpful whenever you are likely to forget. A tape recorder provides such a record at least as accurately as a stenographer.

Cheque-book Manager

The cheque-book money manager is essentially a pocket calculator that keeps track of two charge accounts and credit cards at the same time. You enter a deposit, payment, charge or cheque with a single keystroke. The device keeps an accurate account balance as well as a grand total across all accounts between uses.

Credit Card Alarm

This device appears to be a wallet or a credit card holder, but it is more than that. When the holder is opened and a credit card removed, an alarm is set. If the owner closes the holder without inserting the credit card back in the holder, an alarm will go off, alerting the owner that he or she has yet to get the credit card back from the merchant. This device can help avoid the agony of losing a credit card.

External Knowledge Sources

A special form of back-up for memory records is external knowledge. This kind of back-up consists of information in books, magazines and on computer files that would otherwise have to be learned, retained and remembered. For example, we are not really expected to remember many of the things we learned in school or at work . Instead, we look things up because we no longer remember what we once knew. Similarly, we do not expect ourselves to remember all of the details of experiences that were once fresh in our minds. Nevertheless, we sometimes need information about our past.

To back up your memory on topics you are likely to forget, you need to keep external knowledge sources such as diaries and notebooks. Research indicates that very successful people keep more back-up records and external knowledge sources than less successful people.

Medication Reminders

People who have to take medication find active medication reminders invaluable. Such devices require the patient to put the medication into a separate box with several compartments and to set a timer that triggers an alarm as a reminder to take the medication at the appropriate time.

Personal Data Assistants

Several companies make devices that record personal data used in everyday life: appointments, phone numbers and memos, for instance. These devices remind a person of his or her daily schedule. They display the times of an appointment and who is to be met.

Organizers

Losing things is one of the most annoying of memory problems. When we put an object somewhere it is such an ordinary act that we frequently don't pay attention to what we are doing. The simplest way to avoid losing things is consistently to put them in the same place – in drawer organizers or files, for example. Later, when you want to find something, the organization does the remembering for you.

Notes

Stick a reminder to yourself in a spot where you can't help but see it – on the front door, a frequently used mirror or your television, refrigerator or bathroom door. Adhesive notes are convenient, easy to use and handy. A message board on the wall can remind you of things you have to do. Unfortunately, people get so used to the message board that they forget to look at it. Adhesive notes are often found to be useful to older people, perhaps living alone, or who do not have partners to remind them what to do.

Possession Tags

We all misplace our possessions from time to time, and even when the possession is found, we may not be sure if it is ours. The problem is often acute when collecting luggage after a plane has landed as many pieces of luggage look identical. The solution to this problem is to mark the articles in a conspicuous manner, attaching a bright ribbon or length of yarn to the items or even fastening name labels to them.

The 'Memory-friendly' Office

The ease with which people learn and remember partly depends on the organization of the environment in which they work and their familiarity with this organization. When people work under high pressure they often have to try to remember the location of a misplaced folder, contract or some other piece of information. You can help yourself by putting the items you use everyday – pens, stapler, tape and so on – on top of the desk so that they will be handy. Similarly, always place your envelopes, letterhead sheets and stationery supplies in the same place on your desk or in a particular drawer.

Memory Robot

This kind of external aid remembers for you. For example, an automatic coffee-maker has a clock that can be set to switch itself on and start making coffee. No one in the home has to remember to make the coffee – instead the machine does it. The automatic coffee-maker acts here like a robot and performs the task for you. Other devices that perform a memory task for you include VCRs that will record a television programme for you when you are not at home or are asleep; systems that will turn the lights on and off in a house while you are away; and systems that will water your lawn when you are not thinking about it. More such devices will no doubt become available in the future.

Memory Corrector

Some devices help people to correct a memory error. Key-rings that beep when you clap or shout overcome the problem of forgetting where you put the keys. A memory corrector corrects a memory error before others may detect it or in time for the consequences of the error to be avoided. At present there are only a few products that function in this way.

Car Finder

Everyone has had the experience of not knowing where he or she parked the car in the huge parking lots of some out-of-town stores. This problem is worse when you are searching for your car at night, when the situation can be especially frustrating or even dangerous. An electronic solution to this problem is a device that sends a signal to your car when a button is pressed on a remote-control device. The radio signal causes the car's lights to blink and its horn to sound, signalling the car's position in the parking lot. The remote-control device is about the size of a pocket calculator and can easily be carried in a pocket or purse.

Key Finders

As noted above, there are a variety of key-rings that can be attached to keys and that make an audible alarm, such as a beep, when the key-ring receives a certain signal. For some, the signal is the sound make by clapping the hands; for another, whistling will make the key-ring beep. Unfortunately, the alarm in the whistle- and sound-activated key-rings is often set off by noises and whistles not made by the owner of the keys. Another, more expensive key-ring triggers the alarm with a radio wave that is sent by pressing a button on a hand-held device. People find the keys easily once they hear the beeping.

All these devices quickly lead the user to the misplaced object. They are also useful for finding other possessions, such as your wallet, cheque-book or medication case, and indeed anything that may be easily misplaced. This radio-activated key-ring can be used to reduce the frustration of searching for lost articles.

Iron with Memory

A hazard for many people lies in ironing clothes. If the iron is put face down and the user gets distracted and goes somewhere else – to answer the phone for example – there is a real danger of a fire. There are a couple of brands of iron now available that have a safety shut-off switch, which is activated when the iron remains flat and motionless for thirty seconds.

Memory Trainers

One kind of memory helper is the teaching machine. These devices are intended to facilitate learning, and modern variants of teaching machines involve devices that attempt to simulate job experience – flying an airplane, navigating a ship, air traffic control and many other occupations. Microcomputer stores stock shelf after shelf with instructional schemes and programs on a wide variety of topics that help learning, including, of course, how to use microcomputers. There are programs that will help you learn a skill like typing, or a foreign language, and there are even some programs that promise to improve your memory!

Memory Measurer

Currently there are no products available that can test your memory in the same way that a thermometer can test your temperature. Nevertheless, there are some products that can be used as a way of measuring, such as hand-held automated games that rely on memory performance. The Simon Game, for example, is marketed as a tester of memory. People who are concerned about their memory can test themselves periodically with the game, and if their performance deteriorates, this alerts them to the need to ask their doctor about their memory.

Some people use a pocket speller for the same purpose. If they discover that they cannot spell words that they used to spell correctly or that it is becoming difficult to learn new spellings, they may want to check on this change in their memory.

Memory Art

Perhaps the oldest aid to memory is art. In the past, paintings and drawings and sketches were sometimes designed by artists specifically to help people use the mental strategy – the method of loci – discussed in Chapter 2. The method of loci involves learning a list of items by mentally placing each item in different rooms of a familiar building. You can do the same thing by mentally placing imagined objects to be learned on selected spots on a picture of a landscape in your home or office. Repeat the placements several times to yourself. When you need to 'retrieve' the list, mentally travel over the landscape from region to region, 'picking up' the items as you go. No one will know why your memory is so good at home or in your office.

Memory Awakeners

Research shows that people are less inclined to get depressed when they can remember their lives. A good way to stay in touch with your past is a diary. It provides a back-up record of events and it also fosters a better memory for events because making a record makes you review what has happened. Another good way to feel connected with your past is to collect mementoes. They remind us of our past and help us remain true to who we think we are. This is especially true of photographs, and keeping photos of yourself and those you love will provide you with powerful cues to remembering your past.

Superstitious Memory Aids

Sometimes people use certain objects superstitiously as external aids. They believe that certain objects have the power to influence memory on the basis of their belief that the object brought them good luck in past memory tasks. Some students wear a special article of clothing, like a 'thinking cap', when they sit examinations because they did especially well while wearing the same cap in the past. Other students will use a 'lucky pen' or bring their books even to closed-book exams. Their superstitious behaviour is not altogether without scientific basis, because the lucky object may put the person in a relaxed state that elicits good test-taking habits. If you have a 'lucky' item, use it.

Help with Forgetting

Finally, this review of memory aids would not be complete without a reference to a type of device that is intended to hinder memory. Instead, when you need to forget information, remove it from view and 'shred it'. By shredding it, you will make it easier to forget it – or at least no one else will be able to know what you know.

Situations Where Memory Aids are Especially Helpful

Shopping
Shopping can be helped by a variety of external aids. There are devices to help you remember to purchase certain things, to note what you have spent and to remember to get your credit card back

from a shop assistant. The external aids you can use for these tasks include a check-list of the groceries most people buy regularly and a cheque-book calculator to keep track of how much you spend. To remember to get your credit card back from a shop assistant, use a card case with a built-in alarm.

Remembering to Take Medication
So that you are certain to remember to take medicine, and which medicine to take, organized pill boxes that have slots for the days of the week or for times during the day can be used. If you prefer a stronger reminder to take your pills, buy a pill box with an alarm.

Obligations and Appointments
The best way to deal with these memory burdens is to use a record system that will help you keep track of your appointments. For many people, the primary record system is an appointment book, and there are dozens of different kinds available. Keep a few memo pads in key places around your house or office – in the kitchen, by your bed and in your car – so that you can jot down obligations as you make them. If you wait until later, you may forget. If you are concerned that forgetting certain appointments will be critical to your job prospects, get yourself a personal data assistant that will beep you when your appointments arrive.

Remembering What You Were Doing
There is no need to purchase an aid for this task. Simply pick up a small object and carry it until you have done whatever you intended to do.

Deciding Whether to Use a Memory Device

Memory devices help enormously with a wide variety of tasks: they lessen your memory burden; and they free your mind so that you can concentrate on things in your life of greater value to you.

Appointment books, memo pads, calendars, check-lists, notes, knowledge sources, teaching machines, memory art, superstitious objects, timing devices, symbolic reminders, labels, a consistent 'take-away' spot, memory-friendly appliances, solid organization and many more external aids are available to you. Imagine how much easier a person's life becomes when he or she uses most or all of these aids. As the following list indicates, you can make the effort to use your memory or you can let a memory device help you.

Memory Devices

BULLETIN BOARD	HOME-REPAIR BOOK
CALENDAR	FILING CABINET
DIARY	ADDRESS BOOK
FINANCIAL RECORD	CALCULATOR
MEMO PAD	MAP
TAPE RECORDER	OBJECT ORGANIZER
SHOPPING LIST	WEATHER SERVICE
PHOTOGRAPH ALBUM	ALARM CLOCK
TELEPHONE NUMBER FILE	APPOINTMENT REMINDER
MEMENTO	MEDICATION REMINDER
DICTIONARY	TIMER
ENCYCLOPAEDIA	KEY FINDER
RECIPE BOOK	

It is important to recognize that different people have different tastes in external aids. Age, for example, seems to be a factor that influences what memory aids are appealing. The table opposite shows how young, middle-aged and elderly people rated the effectiveness of different aids. There are probably several other factors that affect your taste in memory aids, so you should select aids for yourself on the basis of what you think will suit you, and disregard the advice of others.

Mean Usefulness Ratings for Commercial Memory Aids

AID	OLDER	MIDDLE AGE	YOUNG
1. IRON WITH MEMORY	3	4	4
2. TAPE RECORDER	2	3	4
3. WHISTLING TEAPOT	4	3	3
4. CAR MEMO-PAD	2	3	3
5. PARTS CABINET	4	3	3
6. ELECTRONIC MEMO-PAD	2	2	3
7. COFFEE MAKER	3	2	4
8. BOOKMARK	4	3	3
9. PLANT ALARM	4	3	3
10. MEMO STICKERS	3	4	4

Note: A rating of 1 indicated not useful; and a rating of 7 indicated extremely useful. These ratings were drawn from those made for different commercial memory aids, as reported by Petro, Herrmann & Burrows (1991).

It has been suggested that the use of external aids reduces the memory skills that are being aided, because the aid relieves the user of the need to employ such skills. However, it can also be suggested that the use of an aid makes one *more* aware of memory abilities and, hence, more sensible in using them. Regardless of such controversies, enthusiasm about the worth of external aids has steadily grown. You will find memory aids in stationery stores, department stores and electronics stores, and they are available from mail order companies.

Many memory problems need not be solved solely by learning mental strategies. Instead, you can meet your memory needs by the use of a memory device. Because objects and sounds have a big impact on memory, memory devices have a powerful effect on your mind. These devices provide immediate solutions to problems that occur often, if not every day, and this chapter has reviewed the range of memory aids available today.

Examinations and Memory

These days, people of all ages go to school and college and attend training sessions of one kind or another. One of the most useful things that memory aids can do, therefore, is to help people with their examinations. Of course, examinations are about understanding your subject, but the examiner can mark only what is in front of him or her, and if you cannot remember what it is you understand, you will not do well in examinations!

First Letter Memory Aid

One of the most useful memory aids for examinations is the first letter memory aid. This involves learning the first letter of points you wish to use in the examination. For example, in order to remember the colours of the rainbow, you might learn the phrase *R*ichard *o*f *Y*ork *g*ave *b*attle *i*n *v*ain – red, orange, yellow, green, blue, indigo, violet. Sometimes the phrase is shortened to the nonsense word, 'roygbiv'. As noted in Chapter 11, being given the first letter of a word you cannot recall can increase the chances of that word coming back to you by about 50 per cent. Using the first letter, therefore, is an effective way of overcoming a memory block, and in examinations, when you are under stress, it is much more likely that such memory blocks will occur.

Medical students often use this technique in order to remember facts about anatomy, and indeed a book has been published for giving a large number of mnemonic phrases – for example, 'May I Softly Squeeze Charlie's girl?' gives the order of the superior thyroid artery – muscular; infrahyoid, superior laryngeal; Sternomastoid, Cricothyroid; Glandular. Medical students need to learn hundreds of these facts, and next time you have an operation, just pray that your doctor remembers the right memory aid!

A number of studies have shown that using the first letter strategy for well-learned material considerably increases the memory for items and for the order that items are learned in. It is not clear that the first letter strategy is useful when material has not been well learned in the first place. When you prepare for examinations, however, it is generally well-learned material that you want to remember. Often, for example, you want to talk about a number of key points on a particular topic. As soon as you remember the key point, you know you can write about the subject for some time, before moving on to the next key point, which gives you more material to talk about, and so on. For example, in an examination you might be asked a question on the advantages and disadvantages of capital punishment for murder. You might have decided these are:

Advantages

D – 1. Deterrent (makes others less likely to commit same crime)

R – 2. Retribution (justice for victims)

C – 3. Cost (saves state money)

S – 4. Safety (murderer cannot escape to kill again)

Disadvantages

M – 1. Mistakes (cannot be corrected)

R – 2. Rehabilitation (chance to redeem a person)

B – 3. Barbaric (state becomes a killer)

The phrase you might use for advantages is <u>D</u>ead <u>R</u>obbers <u>C</u>an't <u>S</u>lay; the phrase you might use for disadvantages is <u>M</u>istakes <u>R</u>eally <u>B</u>leed. Once you remember the D stands for deterrence, you can then write all you know about deterrence before you go on to the next point, retribution, and so on. The first letter aid does not help you to give a good answer on deterrence, but it does help you to remember to talk about deterrence before moving on to the next point, and so on. What often causes problems in examinations is remembering the points you know very well, but just can't remember under examination pressure. It is exactly in this kind of situation that the first letter memory aid comes into its own and exam success can be achieved with the right kind of preparation.

How, then, should the first letter memory aid be used? In the first place, like aspirin, the system is not good for everyone. Some people find it difficult to make a good phrase or nonsense word. If it takes you a long time and you don't seem to get better with practice, don't use it. Many people, however, have no problem in making first letter memory aids. If you do want to use them for examinations, you are likely to want to remember large numbers of phrases and words for different examinations and different topics, and the possibility that some phrases will get mixed up with others is very high. So that you remember all the memory aid phrases and the points you want to make, we suggest that when you are studying for examinations, you adopt the following strategy.

1. Read through all the relevant material for the topic you are preparing, making note of all the main points.
2. When you have read enough, read through the material to make sure you have understood it.
3. Consider what you think about the topic.
4. Make notes on how you are going to answer, thinking about the main facts some time before the exam.
5. About two weeks before the examination, pick out the main points – perhaps ten or twelve – which you can split into groups.

6. Make up one or two mnemonic phrases or words for each topic.
7. Make sure that they are well learned and that what each letter stands for is well learned.
8. The evening before the examination, go over all the relevant memory aids and what each letter of the memory aid stands for, until your memory for the memory aids, and the keywords they stand for, is perfect.
9. Arrive at the examination room half an hour before the examination starts. Don't talk to anyone, but go over the memory aids and the keywords again.
10. On entering the examination room, look at the examination paper, then write down all the memory phrases and the keywords of the question you are going to answer. That way you do not have to worry about forgetting the memory aid during the examination!

This approach can be useful for school examinations, and even for high level university examinations. One student (MO), who received a first class honours degree, was interviewed immediately after her examinations. It had been suggested to the student that she use the first letter mnemonic aid after she had been found crying during her second examination. The interview went as follows:

Would you say that using mnemonics gives you more confidence?

Yes certainly. Because I started doing it, because for the first few exams I didn't use it at all and I was just a nervous wreck because I could not remember anything and I knew I had learnt things. And I got into the exam and couldn't remember.

What were those first few papers?

Oh, the Abnormal paper and then the Basic Processes and Social. And it was only in the Social I started. I only used one mnemonic for that, that's when I started because I knew I could not get anywhere if I didn't start to make a conscious effort to remember things. Because in the beginning, I said, 'Oh, how silly. I am not using those things', and then I found I could not remember anything so I got home and said 'Right, make up some mnemonics' and it worked.

Did you use them before?

I used them in school sometimes, but I used to think, 'Oh, you've gone past that stage now', but it's amazing you haven't, it does give you a lot of confidence, because you can go in, write them down, and you feel that you are ready to write an answer.

The importance of this interview is that it suggests that one of the main advantages of using memory aids is that it gives users confidence that they will remember what they want to. This, in turn, is likely to reduce the stress of examinations and make it more likely that students will remember even without any memory aids!

There are other advantages of using this approach. One of the main ones is that it forces you, however lazy you are, to read, to think out and to organize your thoughts about a topic. You have to do this in order to end up with points you want to remember. You cannot get a good examination mark if you haven't done the work or don't understand what you have studied, but memory aids can help you to remember what it is you have done and what it is you do understand.

Many teachers and learners think that using memory aids is a low-level activity, and that if you really understand something you will be able to remember it without using memory aids. Even the student interviewed above started out thinking that using memory aids was 'silly'! She quickly discovered, however, that it is much sillier not to remember what you know and understand, under the stress of the examination. It is everybody's experience that the minute we leave the examination hall, we remember all the clever things we should have said but forget in the heat of the moment. What memory aids do is make it more likely that we will remember these points during the examination.

It is also sometimes suggested that using the approach we are suggesting makes students prepare pat answers rather than think during the examination about the questions that are set. We would argue that learners should think about the topics they have studied before they get into the examination. They should know what they think about capital punishment or the causes of the American Civil War or whatever topic they are studying, before they are asked about it in an examination. Of course, preparation should be flexible enough to allow the student to answer according to the 'slant' of the question, but our advice to learners is that it is too late to think in an examination. You should do your thinking *before* you get into the examination.

The more you have to sit and think before and during your writing an answer during an exam, the less time there will be to write, and the less depth you are likely to reach in your answer. Of course, we are overstating the argument somewhat. You have to think about what the examination question is asking and then about what you know in order to answer it. But the main point remains the same. Unless you have prepared well before the examination, so that you know what you are going to write about a particular topic, you will often not do as well as you might. At the least, for individuals who find that they have problems remembering all the topics that they have covered for examinations, it is worth trying the first letter mnemonic strategy.

Peg System and Examinations

Some people, especially those with good visual imagery, prefer to use imagery aids for examinations. The peg system for example, which was discussed in Chapter 2, can be adapted for use in examinations. In some subjects students learn the names of experimenters or characters they want to write about, because as soon as they remember the name, they know then what they want to say about what that person did. For example, suppose the first three experimenter's names are Boyle, Hook and Currie. If you used the peg system, you could remember these names by:

1 = Bun – Boil: You remember a *bun* with a big *boil* on top.
2 = Shoe – Hook: You imagine a *shoe* hanging on a *hook*
3 = Tree – Currie: You imagine eating an Indian *curry* under a *tree* (*curry* is a substitute word for *Currie*).

You can remember key points this way, rather than names of people, of course, and you can use the same method for remembering key points in speeches, as discussed in Chapter 3.

Otherwise, the same rules apply to using the peg system as to the first letter system. You must prepare well before the exam, but you must make sure that you remember what each peg word is linked to for each point about two weeks before the examination, then the night before, then just before the examination. For both systems, try it out before the examinations to make sure it works for you.

Spider Diagrams

Spider diagrams have been proposed by Tony Buzan as a means of both organizing your thoughts on a topic and remembering the points you wish to make in an examination. An example of a spider diagram is shown opposite.

The present authors could find no independent scientific studies of the spider diagram method published in the normal scientific literature. This does not mean, however, that the spider diagram is of little value. On the contrary, a survey carried out in a large class of first year students found that over 70 per cent used spider diagrams for helping their studying and as a memory aid in examinations, and most of the students found spider diagrams useful in helping with their studies. One reason there are no reported studies in the literature may be that it is very difficult to set up an experiment that compares the spider diagram approach with other approaches to see how successful each is as an aid to thinking. Furthermore, statistical

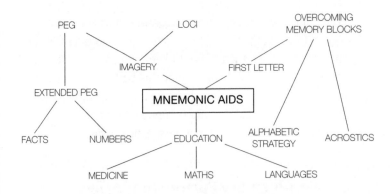

analysis may not be very useful for you, since if an approach works for you, it does not matter if it does not work for, say, 50 per cent of people who perhaps find imagery more difficult than you do. As with all the other memory aids suggested, try it for yourself. If it works for you, use it.

Remembering for Examinations

While it is true that using memory aids can help enormously in examinations, it is also true that memory aids cannot turn a poor student into a good student. Only hard work and understanding can do that. The more you read about a topic, the more ideas you get and the more depth your answer can have. When you read, you should always take notes for two good reasons. First, taking notes makes you think actively about what you are reading; otherwise, you end up at the bottom of the page not able to remember a thing that has gone before. You should take notes only of the major, important points you are reading. It is no use just copying from one book to another. Where possible, put what you have read in your own words, which forces you to think about what you have read, although sometimes you might want to quote an author accurately. The second reason for taking notes is that if you do not, you will soon forget what you have read. If you have made notes, you can read through them before deciding how you want to tackle a problem.

Once you have worked on a topic you should go over it a day later, then a week later, then a month later and so on. As we saw in Chapter 5, research has shown that this pattern of revision is more effective than others. Think about the topic each time you read through it, and try to organize your thoughts so that one idea flows into another, although this may not always be possible.

Non-memory Factors that Affect Memory Performance

How well you do in remembering things for examinations does not just depend on how much work you have done. A large number of non-memory factors also affect memory performance. These include your physical state, your mental state, your surroundings and your social relationships. These were discussed in earlier chapters, but as far as examination preparation is concerned, the findings show that it is useful, if possible, to have a good night's sleep before an examination, but not with the aid of drugs, which could have the opposite effect to the one intended. Do not eat a large meal before an examination. Glucose may help you to perform better on some memory tasks, but it is not clear that it helps in examinations, when you are already likely to be highly aroused. On the other hand, it is unlikely that taking a glucose drink an hour or so before an exam will do you any harm, and since there is some evidence that rising glucose levels improve memory performance in some tasks, we would not, given the information currently available, discourage anyone from taking such a drink. On the other hand, drinking alcohol the night before the examination is not a good idea, and some medications can make you sleepy when you need to be alert.

It is obviously easier said than done, but try to reduce stress. To a large extent, of course, the best stress reducer is the knowledge that you know your material and can remember what you need to know.

Finally, try out a variety of approaches on yourself before the examination and choose one that works for you. Use the methods previously described, and consider carefully all the points discussed in Chapter 5 on the whole-person approach to memory improvement. There is no magic formula that can bring success if you have not done the work or understood the material and thought about it. What memory aids and a whole-person approach can do is help you to perform at your best.

In summary, this chapter has shown how you can prepare for examinations by using a number of different methods, such as the first letter strategy, the peg system, spider diagrams and so on. Only *you* can decide which system works for you. In addition however, successful examination performance depends on doing the work, thinking about it and organizing the material before you go into the exam. Just as important for good examination performance is to pay attention to non-memory factors, such as your physical state and your mental state. Luck is an element in examinations, but the harder you work on the points discussed in this chapter, the luckier you are likely to be.

The 'Tip-of-the-tongue' Experience and Memory Blocks

We have all had the experience of being certain that we know something, but not being able to recall it. We often describe the word we are looking for as being 'on the tip-of-the-tongue', and often the experience can be both embarrassing and frustrating. It is embarrassing if the word we are looking for is the name of a friend we have just met by chance; it is frustrating because we get irritated with ourselves and keep trying to get the word back – sometimes for days!

As we get older we get more tip-of-the-tongue experiences, but this is not necessarily because we are older. It seems to be that tip-of-the-tongue experiences occur for something that was well learned at one time but has not been used for a while. Even younger people get tip-of-the-tongue experiences for books they have not read for ten years or for old school friends. The older you are, the more material you will have stored that you knew some time ago but have not used for a while. You can usually generate a tip-of-the-tongue experience for yourself. Just picture your old school teachers or your old school friends or the authors of books you have read about ten years ago. Sooner or later you are likely to get a tip-of-the-tongue experience.

The tip-of-the-tongue phenomenon is a bit of a mystery. If we know something well enough to be certain we know it, why is it not coming back? What is it we know we know, if we know we know something well enough to know that we know it, but can't get it back? A more important question perhaps is whether there is anything we can do to help overcome the memory block that is giving us the tip-of-the-tongue experience? The answer is yes, at least some of the time.

The first thing to remember if you have a tip-of-the-tongue experience is that most of them resolve themselves quite quickly without too much effort on your part. However, if the answer does not pop into your mind in a few seconds, the best thing to do is to keep trying to get it back. One study of the tip-of-the-tongue experience found that some answers came after more than a minute, but this is a long time to try to get an answer when you are in a tip-of-the-tongue state. If, after a minute or so, the answer still has not come back, the next stage is to leave it alone – stop thinking about it – for an hour or even longer. Then go back to the problem and try to remember what the answer is.

One study found that only when people went back to a question, to try to remember the answer, did more answers come. In other words, when you have a tip-of-the-tongue experience, it is not clear that answers pop up spontaneously. Even when people report that answers just pop up, it might well be that they have gone back to thinking about the answer, which then comes so quickly that they don't even realize they have turned back again to think about it!

What kinds of thing should you do when you are trying to think about an answer? One study found that in about 50 per cent of cases, where you are certain you know an answer but cannot get it back, then being given the first letter of a missing answer will result in your recalling the correct answer. This is a clue to one way of proceeding if you find you have a memory block. Go through the alphabet slowly, one letter at a time, in order to see if each letter might be the first letter of the missing word. So you ask yourself, does the word begin with an A, a B, a C and so on. Often the word you are looking for pops up even if it does not start with the letter you have reached. For example, when you are on B, it might be that the word you are looking for – say, Helsinki – pops into your mind. One study found that in about 25 per cent of cases where someone has a tip-of-the-tongue experience, using this alphabetic method results in recall. In examinations. or when you are trying desperately to remember someone's name, these are pretty good odds.

The alphabet strategy is not the only way to help you find your missing memories. As well as going through the alphabet, you should try to remember as many things you can about the missing memory. If it is an old school friend whose name you can't remember, for example, try to remember the names of other friends at the time; try to remember the name of his or her boy- or girlfriend; whether you had an argument; where the friend went after leaving school; whether there was a nickname, and so on. If you are trying to remember a word, try to think of the number of syllables, whether it is a common word or an uncommon word – think of as many things about the word as you can. As we said before, if this does not work, leave it for a while, then go back and use these strategies again. Often the word comes back quickly the second time you try to get it.

Until now we have been talking of the tip-of-the-tongue phenomenon, when not only are you certain you know something, but this feeling often goes with being certain that the word is just not coming. In fact, however, one of the strange things about memory is that we know the contents of our memories even before we get the words out. We can be in a tip-of-the-tongue state, when we are certain we know something but be irritable because we can't produce it. We can be equally certain we don't know something. Do you know the meaning of the word 'santifax'? You are probably certain you don't know it – in fact, there is no such word, but the interesting thing is that you know straight away that you don't know it – it does not ring any bells! On the other hand you may know something and not be in a tip-of-the-tongue state. Your feeling of knowing might vary from being sure you know something that you can't get back, to thinking you know something, to being sure you don't know something, and many studies have shown that we are quite accurate about our assessment of what is in our memory store, even though we cannot get the word back. If we are sure we know it, we are much more likely to get the word back later on than if we only think we know it. How on earth can we be sure we know something (and be correct about our feeling) without getting the actual word back? There are probably at least two reasons. First, often when we have a tip-of-the-tongue state, another similar word keeps coming into our head, suggesting that this 'wrong' word is blocking our ability to get the right word out. Second, we might know that we know so much about the missing word – for example, the names of all our other friends – that we must know the name of our missing friend. Whatever the reason, the important thing is that there are things we can do to help ourselves when we can't get the word we want.

The most common situation in which memory blocks occur is when trying to remember someone's name, particularly when we are under stress, such as in examinations. What, then, should you do if you are talking to someone and cannot remember his or her name? First, keep talking in the hope that something they say will trigger an association that will lead to the name! It is usually more embarrassing to get the name wrong than to omit to say the name. Occasionally, using the face–name associative strategy results in remembering a substitute name, such as sex for Sykes, for example, but if you have gone over names recently this almost never happens. One thing you should try to avoid is introducing people to each other when you have forgotten the name of one of them, even if you feel that by not introducing them, you are making it obvious you have forgotten a name.

The other main situation in which memory blocks occur is under the stress of examinations. In Chapter 10 on memory and examinations we discussed ways in which you can reduce the probability of blocks occurring in the first place.

In summary, this chapter has looked at the really annoying feeling we get when something is on the tip of our tongue but we cannot get it back. In order to get to the tip-of-the-tongue memory, first keep trying to get it back for even as long as a minute – it often comes back after quite a long time. Second, if this fails, leave it alone for a period of time then try again. When trying to get a word back, go through the alphabet one letter at a time to see if this helps. Try to remember as many things as you can about the missing word, when you saw it last, how big it was, whether it was a long or a short word and so on. Many memory blocks are overcome.

Remembering to Do Things

To do or not to do; these are the options. Unfortunately, carrying out these options can occur only if you remember what it is you want to do!

There are many things that we have to remember to do. Everyone has appointments to make, deadlines to meet, appliances to stop and start, meetings to go to, birthdays to celebrate, letters to post, errands and chores to do. In conversation, we have points we intend to make. As we leave home, we often have to remember to pick up things we will need where we are going. When we are to go on a trip, we must remember to pack all the items we will need.

Remembering to do things depends on what is called *prospective memory*. This kind of memory keeps records of things we intend to do: appointments, meetings, chores, deadlines, social engagements and so on. Each record stores two pieces of information. First, the record stores the future act that has to be done. Second, the record stores a cue that – when it appears – signals to a person that an act has to be carried out. For example, if we have to pick up someone at 3pm, a cue to go to our car and pick the person up may be when our watch shows 2:45pm.

Remembering to do things is often the most difficult of memory tasks, because many actions have to be executed at a certain time or within a certain interval. If you fail to remember to perform an intended act on time or before the interval is completed, other people might well feel that your prospective memory has failed. Being just

Your Memory for Life!

a little late for an appointment will often be forgiven but often it will not be forgotten.

Prospective memory failures can often put people in professional, as well as personal, difficulty. When you forget an appointment with another person, his or her schedule is disrupted and this disruption is often sufficient to make many people angry. A forgotten appointment may offend, and many people feel that a failure to meet an appointment means a lack of affection and/or respect. After all, if the other person were really important to you, you would remember.

Forgetting to do something has a similar effect to that produced by forgetting an appointment. When someone forgets a chore that others depend on, such as collecting the bread, others judge the forgetter as not 'responsible'. If the chore affects the plans of others, such as forgetting to bring the drinks for a picnic, those affected may get annoyed. Professionally, failures to meet certain appointments or execute certain tasks can destroy chances for a promotion or even put someone's employment at risk. In the military, failures to carry out chores can be regarded as an offence and lead the forgetter in to real trouble, because lives sometimes depend on remembering to bring the right medicine, equipment and so on.

How Prospective Memory Works

Memory aids of the kinds discussed in Chapters 1 and 2 have been in use over two thousand years. Science has only investigated memory for just over a hundred years, and surprisingly, memory for future actions has been investigated for less than twenty years. Because of this, not all that much is known yet about memory for future actions – that is, prospective memory.

At least three explanations have been offered for prospective memory. One explanation is that people associate a cue – a light, a sound, an object, a feeling – in the environment to what they want to do at the same time as they commit to memory their intention to do something. Later they remember what they are supposed to do when the cue occurs again in the environment – for example, the clock striking three reminds the parent to pick up the child. If a cue arrives too late, it is obviously useless, but cues that arrive too early may be forgotten before they can act as cues. According to the cue explanation, therefore, you will be most likely to remember your intentions if you arrange for the critical cue to arrive at the appropriate time. If you remind yourself to take things to work, say, by putting them right in front of your front door, you are using the cue method to remember to do things.

A second explanation of how we remember to do things in the future assumes that people remain aware of the passing of time by noting what has been happening in their lives. After deciding to do something in the future, more and more events occur as one nears the time of the intended action. When a person senses that a sufficient amount of time has passed, he or she knows that it is time to carry out the action. For example, if you decide it is time to go to an appointment shortly after lunch by recalling that you have just had lunch, you are using the inference method – that is, inferring from events that have gone before that it is time to meet the appointment.

A third explanation holds that people have a biological clock that makes them conscious that it is time to perform an intended act. The existence of the biological clock is widely accepted – for example, a biological clock is believed to wake us up when we do not use an alarm clock. Whether it is involved in prospective memory is not known, but it is plausible that the same part of our mind that awakes us is also involved in making us aware of time. If you find yourself thinking it must be late in the day and you should pick your children up from school, it may be that your biological clock made you aware of the time. It does, however, seem as if our biological clock is also affected by cues in the environment. Research has shown that people who live in the absence of any cues about the time of day develop their own.

You might be wondering why psychologists would bother with these explanations when most people wear a wristwatch or can see a clock to tell them the time. The answer is that we look at a clock when we suspect that we may have something to do. Thus, the explanations of *how* we remember what we do also explain *why* we look at a watch or clock.

You might also be wondering why there should have to be all these explanations when people can set an alarm to remind them. We agree that alarms can be very helpful reminders and Chapter 9 describes all manner of devices that remind and help memory in other ways. However, not everyone uses alarms as reminders, and people who do so do not use alarms to remind them of everything they do. Also, sad to say, many people still forget to do the intended act after having been reminded by an alarm. Therefore, people must rely on cues, inference and biological reminders whether they like it or not if they are to be sure of successfully carrying out future intentions.

Kinds of Intention

As suggested earlier, there are different kinds of intention. Some intentions require the act to be completed at a precise time. These intentions are time-based – appointments are time-based, and deadlines that must be met at one's work are time-based. Time-based intentions require attention to time cues.

Other intentions do not require the act to be completed at any particular time. Chores often have to be completed on a vague, unspecified schedule, and we often do them when some event reminds us to do so. Weeding the garden might be an example of such a chore, and the event might be your partner becoming frustrated at the sight of the garden becoming overrun with weeds.

Intentions also differ according to how often they must be done. Many intended acts are habitual – brushing one's teeth, mowing the lawn, for example – and habitual intentions are easier to remember than intentions that are carried out just once, such as meeting a salesperson to buy a car. There is evidence that the amount of practice that the person has had with prospective memory tasks improves the remembering of that task.

Regrettably, cues, inferences and the biological clock are often not up to prospective memory tasks. People often forget the things they have to do, and interruptions to one's daily routine can throw inferences about the time completely off course. Cues sometimes do not look the same as when the intention was committed to memory – for example, you might use a television programme as a cue to remind yourself of something to be done. However, if you have forgotten to switch on the television, obviously it will not give you the cue you need.

Many factors increase failure at prospective memory tasks. Prospective memory depends on the time of day the intention is to be performed. Typically, people are more likely to remember their appointments earlier rather than later in the day. This effect of time of day on prospective memory is probably due to fatigue, which is known to increase across the day. Anxiety, too, can interfere with remembering what to do, and appointments are often forgotten because thinking about them makes people anxious.

The one single factor that probably helps you most to remember what to do is motivation. The more that you are likely to be rewarded, or the more likely you are to be punished if you forget, the more likely it is that you will not forget the intended action.

Generally, success at remembering the future is less likely the longer you have to remember to do the action – that is, the longer the time between deciding to do something and the time of doing it, the greater the chances are that you will forget to do it. You are more likely to remember to visit your aunt today than in a week's time.

Remembering the future is also less successful if there are other tasks to be performed around the same time. In daily life, it is not uncommon for a person to have more than one task to remember to do at the same time. For example, on leaving for work you may have several things that you will need to remember to do: you may know that you need to bring with you a certain report that you had previously taken home; you may also have to get some petrol for your car, deliver the report to the boss before 9am, have lunch with a colleague, and requisition supplies from the stationery department before 3pm.

People also differ in their ability to perform future memory tasks across their lifespan. Generally, and perhaps surprisingly, this ability increases with age. The explanation for the advantage of age appears to lie in motivation and practice. Young people fail at these tasks because they are neither rewarded as greatly for succeeding nor punished as greatly for failing at prospective tasks. Middle-aged people often cannot afford to fail at prospective tasks or they will risk losing their jobs or gain a reputation among their friends for being unreliable. Older people also do very well at prospective tasks because of the years of practice they have had at prospective memory tasks.

Improving 'Remembering to Do Things'

General Actions

Because of the unfortunate consequences of forgetting appointments and chores, people often arrange to remind themselves rather than expect themselves to remember spontaneously. They do so in a variety of ways, and different prospective tasks call for different procedures.

An essential part of the successful remembering of prospective memories is planning and record keeping. You might, for example, use a two-level system of recording intentions. This system consists of keeping a calendar that keeps all long- and short-range intentions. In addition, you can carry an appointment book or list that keeps just that information you need for what you should do the next day. Review your schedule at least twice a day, and review your calendar once at night to get your short- and long-range plans in mind and to create your next day's list. In the morning refresh yourself for what you have to do by checking your appointment book.

Specific Actions

Intentions that must be carried out at a certain *time* are remembered best with the help of an alarm – see Chapter 9. For example, many kinds of medication must be taken at precise times throughout the day or else the patient may suffer severe, perhaps life-threatening, side effects. Fortunately, reminding devices, such as pill-cap alarms, are available to remind the patient at the necessary times to take medication. A reminding device is recommended for anyone whose health condition is too serious to trust to memory.

If you have arranged an important appointment, make a note about the appointment or meeting as soon as you can after agreeing it. Always keep a record of the things you have to do in an appointment book, calendar, diary, or bulletin board. If you cannot jot down an intention then and there, change something around you, such as tipping a lampshade, putting your watch on the other wrist or placing something on the floor in a conspicuous place – even a knot in your handkerchief. When you come across the 'odd' arrangement, it will have the effect of making you think 'what am I supposed to remember?' Later, you can transfer notes that you remember about new appointments into your appointment book at the first opportunity.

If an appointment is important, it is wise to set an alarm to remind you. If an alarm is not handy or if meeting the appointment is not critical, rely on your memory. A well-known method for developing a good memory for future events is to imagine oneself performing the intended act. The trick is to make the image full of the same cues that are expected to occur in the context in which the act is to be performed. For example, a common way to prepare to remember an appointment is to imagine the person to be met standing alongside a clock at a certain time. Later, when you look at a clock around that time, the image comes to meet the person.

One kind of intention that is difficult to remember is a *birthday*. If you forget, the other person is less likely to recognize that birthdays are hard to remember than to be hurt. It is wise to record birthdays in your calendar or diary as soon as you find out about them. Buy cards for everyone at the beginning of the year, address and sign the cards and file them in appropriate slots of a month-by-month organizer.

When it comes to remembering chores, you have to make an extra effort to remind yourself. Leave out tools – for example, the vacuum cleaner – or carry one of your tools, utensils or materials with you. Avoid being deflected from the chores. Consult a list and cross off items as you get them done. Ask someone to remind you – perhaps the person who asked you to do the chores in the first place.

Deadlines, such as due dates, renewal of licence and insurance forms, are often important. Imagine doing some act that comes immediately before the deadline and associate it with the deadline. When you perform this associated act, it will tend to bring to mind the deadline. Many deadlines must be met on or before a particular time; others must be met on or about a particular time. Some deadlines occur again and again – picking up children after school, for example – and optional intentions may or may not be performed on or about vague deadlines. Obligatory deadlines require more preparation than the optional deadlines, and exact deadlines involve more use of external memory aids, like alarm watches, than other kinds of intention. Appointment books, calendars, diaries, bulletin boards, notes in obvious places – all these help to remind us of exact deadlines.

Remembering to convey a message to someone you know from someone else shows both that you care about them. Forgetting to do so suggests that you don't care about at least one of them. It is crucial that you commit the message to memory in the first place, and this can be especially difficult if you were told the message in a hectic situation. Rehearse the message until you have the chance to write the message down. Ask the source of the message to repeat it, because repetition will impress the message on your memory, especially if you think about its meaning. Set an alarm later to remind you to convey the message.

For many people paying bills is an annoying prospective memory task. Many people write the due dates of bills on their calendar or in a diary. If you get into the habit of reviewing your calendar at least once daily, you will be reminded of the bills, too. Keep important bills in a visible place, to serve as a reminder that they need to be paid. Red bills often act as a good reminder, if one is needed!

We often need to take things we have at home with us to work or somewhere else for social purposes. Probably the best way to be sure you will remember to take something with you is to put it in the front seat of you car (not in the back where it might be forgotten). If you are reluctant to put it in your car ahead of time or if that is not convenient, put the object in front of the door to your home or flat. Some people have a regular spot in their home – a table by the front door or worktop in the kitchen – on which they always place things. One final tip, we often remember to do something when we are lying in bed. Don't rely on remembering what you thought of after you get into bed or in the night or when you get up in the morning. Get out of bed and write down or, better still, have a pad and pen at your bedside to write down what you thought of doing. Alternatively, use the mental filing system described in Chapter 2.

In summary, prospective memory tasks are difficult partly because each one calls for a somewhat different approach to remembering. If you are already performing a particular prospective task well, then forget about that task and concentrate on the tasks that seem to trouble you. Analyse whether the task has to be done by a certain time or when some event occurs – after a phone call, for example. Consider whether you can improve by taking account of cues, by becoming more aware of how you gauge the time and the situation in which the task occurs. Consider whether better self-care of your mental strength or doing something about anxiety might improve your performance. Given that people can get very upset with us if we fail to remember to do things, a little effort to improve our prospective memory can be well worth it.

Memory and the Law

All of us hope that we will never be on the wrong side of the law. However, the chances are that at some time in our lives, we *will* be involved, as members of a jury, as eyewitnesses, as 'innocent' members of a police identification parade or just possibly as someone wrongly accused of a crime. As anyone who has experienced the process will tell you, being an eyewitness can be a terrifying experience, and being a member of a jury puts tremendous responsibility on you to see that justice is carried out.

Apart from the few cases of witness or police dishonesty, by far the greatest problem the legal system faces is human error and procedures that could be much better than they are. Because the efficient working of the legal system is in everyone's interest, it is important to know about the problems and what steps can be taken to help.

Eyewitness Memory Accuracy

It has been known for a long time that, even with the best will in the world, eyewitness memory can, under some circumstances, be very unreliable, even when the witness is certain he or she is giving a truthful and accurate account. A number of factors affect the accuracy of eyewitness, including age, the degree of stress of an event and the expectations that witnesses have about an event.

As far as age is concerned, young children can be good witnesses, but a number of studies have found that they are more susceptible to suggestive or leading questions. This does not mean that their memory for, say, punishment they suffered is not accurate, but care must be taken to ask questions in a way that is not suggestive. Young children also tend to give less full accounts of facts. This does not mean that their evidence should be ignored, nor does it mean it is less accurate, but it does mean that one must be even more careful than with adults that they are not responding to subtle pressures. Young children sometimes recall an event they have witnessed less fully than a young adult. Children are also susceptible to their memories being distorted by events that take place after the event in question, but it must be stressed that this can happen to people of all ages; adults can have their memories distorted by later events, too. Interestingly, there is little evidence that police officers have any special abilities as witnesses.

A range of factors surrounding the witnessed event may make the eyewitness, of whatever age, more or less reliable. It is, for example, almost self-evident that the longer someone has to observe, say the face of a robber, the better will be recognition of that face. Unfortunately, witnesses are very poor at estimating accurately how long they were able to observe an event, and almost all witnesses overestimate the length of an event. One study of a filmed bank robbery found that most people estimated it took about two and a half minutes. In fact, it took only 30 seconds. If witnesses cannot accurately estimate the time they watched an event, it is difficult to estimate how likely they were to have had a good enough view to remember what they saw.

Another problem occurs in stressful situations. When we are under stress we often concentrate on what seems to us the most important aspect of the event, and as a result our memory of what, at the time, seems to us less important aspects tends to be less good. Stress also appears to make eyewitnesses less accurate; at other times there seems to be a flashbulb memory, as in the case of John Kennedy's assassination, so that we seem to be able to remember much better.

After a time, however, even this flashbulb memory can become inaccurate.

Perhaps the most worrying thing about eyewitness memory is that a great deal of evidence shows that events that take place *after* a witnessed event can distort the memory of the original event. One classic American study showed people pictures of a car involved in an accident. The car passed a stop sign just before the accident. Immediately after the accident had been shown, the experimenter mentioned to half the observers that the car had gone through a stop sign; to the other half of the observers the experimenter mentioned a yield sign. Later viewers were asked to say whether they had seen the stop or the 'yield' sign. Where a stop sign had been mentioned after the event (the actual sign seen), 75 per cent reported having seen a stop sign. Where a yield sign had been mentioned after the event, only 41 per cent chose correctly. In other words, viewers were more likely to choose the circumstance they had heard mentioned after the event than the original sign. A large number of other studies have reported similar findings.

There is no doubt, therefore, that what is experienced after an event can very much influence the accuracy of eyewitness memories. However, that finding should be balanced by other findings that show that it tends to be minor points, or points not central to the main event, that are most subject to distortion later on. Nevertheless, some main aspects of events *are* subject to distortion, such as the effects of 'mugshot' memory. It is often the case that in a police investigation, witnesses are shown photographs of suspects. There is considerable evidence that eyewitnesses sometimes pick out in an identity parade the individual whose photograph they have seen and not the actual criminal. In any case, there is often no way of knowing at the time or indeed in court, what the witness regarded as important at the time of viewing. Clearly, as almost all police investigation involves interrogating witnesses (often a long time after an incident), the kind of information that the police give to witnesses, just by the kind of questions that might be asked, is potentially a very dangerous source of witness 'contamination'. Add to that the problem that there is often a very large time gap between police interviews and a court appearance, and it is easy to see how 'fact' and 'suggestions' can become intertwined. It does not mean that they always do.

Recovered Memories and the False Memory Syndrome

One widely discussed topic at present is known as the 'false memory syndrome' or 'recovered memories'. There is considerable evidence from clinical psychologists and therapists that a number of their clients have repressed painful memories from childhood, particularly memories of childhood sexual abuse. Obviously the implications of uncovering long-held memories of this kind are likely to be devastating on family relationships, so the memory of such events is an extremely serious matter. However, there is a great deal of clinical evidence that child sexual abuse does occur. The horrifying events surrounding some recent trials have revealed the horrific sexual abuse of children, who were coerced into thinking that such abuse was 'normal'!

Yet the fact that child sexual abuse does take place does not mean that whenever such memories are 'uncovered' in therapy it must have taken place. There is strong evidence that 'memories' can sometimes be false. One psychologist has extended her work on the unreliability of eyewitness memory to the unreliability of 'recovered' memories. She and others have shown convincingly that it is quite possible to 'plant' memories in individuals, who then become completely convinced they have experienced 'events' that were, in fact, suggested by the experimenter. It is easy to see that some therapists might unwittingly do the same to their clients – 'suggesting' memories of abuse, which the client comes to believe are real. There is also the possibility that sometimes the 'memory' is real, but the interpretation of the memory might be wrong. Almost all parents, for example, bathe their children, and in the course of

119

bathing, clean their genital areas. Although such contact is innocent and harmless, under some circumstances, this contact might be interpreted in a sinister way, for example, by a depressed or unhappy person. So the situation is that repressed memories are likely to constitute a real phenomenon but that some memories may be false. The huge difficulty is to know what is 'real' and what is 'false'. This is not a satisfactory state of affairs. The important point is that such memories, real or not, indicate a person who needs psychological help.

Identification Parades/Line ups

One of the most common ways in which witnesses are used by the police is the identity parade or line-up where witnesses are asked to pick out a suspect from a line of people, all of whom look like the suspect. A great deal of work has shown, however, that many mistakes can be made using the identity parade, although recent studies have shown at least something can be done to reduce the errors.

The first problem concerns the feelings of the witness who is asked to pick out the suspect. If that witness has seen or even been the victim of, say, a violent crime, having to identify a suspect face-to-face is an ordeal. Under stress, the accuracy of memory often declines, so that the very process of identifying a witness may lead to inaccuracies. The introduction of one-way mirrors to avoid direct confrontation is helpful, but even this does not by any means eliminate the stress caused by having to relive part of a traumatic event.

Adding to the problem of stress in the witness is the knowledge that the police feel they have got a good suspect. If they did not, why would they be conducting the identity parade in the first place? Witnesses under stress, therefore, may well choose the nearest match to what they remember, believing that they must be mistaken in some minor detail that doesn't match the chosen suspect. Other factors that are of importance include how similar all the people in the line-up are in appearance. Suppose the suspect was a man, and all but one of the people in the line-up were women. Obviously this would not be fair, since the witness would be eliminating the women but not necessarily identifying the man. This may sound too ridiculous to be true, but, a recent case involved a line-up in which the suspect was a Eurasian of mixed blood, while all the other people in the line-up were Gurkhas from a local Gurkha regiment. An identification was made and the suspect arrested! Of course, few identity parades are as bad as this, but it is still difficult to be sure that the suspect is similar to all the others in a line-up. At the least, a defence lawyer should insist on a photograph of the line-up so that juries can judge how fairly it was conducted.

Another major problem of the identity parade is that many witnesses will have seen mugshots of the suspect who is included in the line-up. As noted earlier, the danger is that the witness will identify the person in the line-up who has been seen in a photograph and is therefore familiar, rather than remember the person as being the person at the scene of the crime. This is another example of information after an event distorting the memory for the original event. One famous study shown just how serious the problem is. A group of 'witnesses' was shown ten 'criminals' for about twenty-five seconds each and told they should look at them carefully as they would have to pick them out from mugshots and from line-ups later. About an hour and a half later, the witnesses were shown fifteen mugshots, some of the 'criminals' and some of new faces. A week later, the witnesses had to pick out the 'criminals' they had seen earlier from a real identity parade. If a person in the identity parade had not been seen earlier, either as a criminal or as a mugshot, he was picked out by witnesses as a criminal on only 8 per cent of occasions. If the person in the identity parade was not one of the criminals, but had been seen in a mugshot, his chances of being mistakenly identified as a criminal rose to 20 per cent.

One extraordinary example of misidentification at an identity parade was the case of an Australian psychologist who was on television discussing violent crime at the very time that a woman was being raped in her home. The woman gave as a description of the rapist that of the psychologist she had seen on television and picked him out in an identity parade as the rapist. There are not many suspects who have as good an alibi as that psychologist, but the evidence is clear. Seeing people who might be linked to a crime after the crime has taken place, even if in photographs, greatly affects the possibility of an innocent person being picked out at an identity parade.

What Can Be Done to Help?

Fortunately, there are things that can be done to make identity parades much fairer, and some police forces are already taking steps in this direction. First, it is important to allow witnesses to view suspects through a one-way mirror, and for police to emphasize that *none* of the people on view might be the guilty person. Second, all defence lawyers should have a picture of the identity parade, so that the likeness of the suspect and the other people on parade can be assessed by the jury. Third, the defence lawyer should establish whether photographs have been viewed before the identity parade. Fourth, and most important, there is strong evidence that if people on parade are presented one at a time, rather than all together in a line, the number of times witnesses pick an innocent person falls by about 30 per cent but they still pick correctly the same percentage of guilty people. Witnesses say 'yes' or 'no' immediately after each individual is presented to them, rather than waiting until the end before making a judgement. The reason this reduces errors is probably that witnesses in normal line-ups feel compelled to make a choice between all the people in front of them. If witnesses see suspects one at a time, they are less likely to choose someone who 'resembles' the suspect until the last person has been seen. If this last person does not resemble the suspect, no choice will be made.

Witnesses to a crime can also help by making it more likely they will remember a face. When you look at someone, you should make judgements about whether someone is nice or nasty, clever or stupid, polite or rude, attractive or unattractive, as well as judging whether the nose is big or small, the eyes close or far apart, the ears big or small, the mouth big or small and so on. The more the face is made distinct, the greater the probability of identifying it correctly later. Some faces are, or course, more distinctive than others, and there is evidence that extremely attractive and unattractive faces are more memorable because they are more distinctive than faces in the middle of the range.

No one is arguing that identity parades are not useful and should not be used in evidence. But it is important to realize that mistakes can be made, and it is also important to realize that just because someone is not identified in a line-up, that person is not necessarily innocent. There may be other good evidence to allow a conviction. It is clear, however, that it is dangerous to convict where the strongest evidence is identification and where other evidence would not lead to conviction, unless, of course, there are unique aspects to a person's appearance that could be known only to a witness, such as a tattoo behind the ear. On the other hand, positive identification by, say, three independent witnesses, *combined* with other strong evidence, is, of course, helpful, but even three independent witnesses are not really enough, since all may be misled by a feature, such as sticking-out ears, that are characteristic of a number of individuals.

The police are under instructions to follow rules that avoid some of the problems we have discussed, but it is difficult to be sure that all the rules have been followed so there is no danger of a false identification taking place. At the least, anyone in a trial that involves eyewitness identification should be aware of the problems involved.

Eyewitness Confidence and Accuracy

Common sense tells us that the more confident a witness is the more likely he or she is to give accurate information. This has sometimes been recognized in courts of law, where the jury is often asked to pay attention to the demeanour of witnesses. Indeed, the confidence of a witness giving evidence is the single most important factor that jurors take into account when they assess the value of a piece of evidence. Sad to say, studies by psychologists completely fail to show any consistent relationship between eyewitness confidence and eyewitness accuracy!

So many studies have been done on this question that there is now no room for doubt. Under some circumstances, there is little or no relationship between the confidence and the accuracy of an eyewitness. There is no relationship if viewing conditions are poor or if witnesses are not given an opportunity to observe the situation for long enough or if there is a high degree of stress or if some aspects of an event are not well observed and so on. The better the viewing conditions, the greater is the likelihood of a relationship between confidence and accuracy. However, even if this is the case, it is sometimes possible for a witness to be confident and yet wrong. One of the present authors conducted a study in which there was an argument between a lecturer and two 'students' in his class, after which the 'students' were asked to leave. They came to the front of the class, and argued with the lecturer for a further twenty seconds in full view of the class. Over 75 per cent of the class were embarrassed, and all but five of 109 students thought the incident was for real. They were then asked different questions about the incident and asked to say how certain they were they were correct. On one point seventeen witnesses were certain they were correct, but only two were, in fact, correct. On the other hand, on another point, of the nine witnesses who were certain they were correct, eight were correct. The more the group as a whole was correct, the more likely were confident individuals to be correct, but clearly in some situations even highly confident individuals are more likely to be wrong than right.

There are, however, many situations where eyewitness confidence and accuracy do go together – asking people what they had for breakfast, for example. In many situations people are confident because there are factors that support their evidence – you might, for example, remember with certainty that an accident happened at 4.45pm, because you left a football match at 4.40pm and had walked for only five minutes when the accident happened. You know the football match ended at 4.40 because it always ends at 4.40. Again, if a witness claims it was her mother she met when shopping, it is highly unlikely that confidence and accuracy would be unrelated! The problems arise when events are fast-moving or surprising, and you have to remember unfamiliar or unusual facts, such as a new face or the colour of someone's shirt. In these cases it is dangerous to rely on an individual's confidence alone.

Improving Eyewitness memory

If the police are going to solve crimes, it is essential that witnesses give investigating officers as much accurate information as possible. As we saw earlier, witnesses are often unable to give all the accurate information that is needed, and it is important that police officers use interview methods that give them as high as level of accurate information as possible. In other words, the way in which an investigating officer asks questions is very important.

How you ask is critical
One study has shown that just small changes in how a question is asked can change the accuracy of recall. One group of witnesses was asked how tall a basketball player was, while another group was asked how short he was. There was an average difference in the replies of eight inches. Obviously, any investigating officer must be careful how questions are asked, and probably the best way to collect information is to ask witnesses to give their own account of events in their own way. This seems to lead to the greatest amount of accuracy.

On many occasions, however, investigating officers tolerate a lot of inaccuracy provided further accurate information is also given. For example, it might be that when they are asked to give further information, which the witnesses may not think important, five further facts come to light, of which four are not useful, but one may be critical in leading to further important information. In such a case, having to eliminate the four irrelevant or inaccurate 'facts' may not be important, and at the investigating stage having more information, even if some of it is inaccurate, might be vital. In court, on the other hand, all the evidence should be accurate.

In order to get more information from witnesses, after they have given their own accounts, the investigating officer can ask more specific questions, which should, ideally, be open-ended and the 'sought for' answer should not be suggested.

'Hypnosis' and the 'Cognitive Interview'

Sometimes, when further information is desperately needed, the police try hypnosis. Courts do not like evidence based on hypnosis, which usually leads to additional wrong as well as accurate information coming out. However, for the purposes of trying to obtain new leads, there is evidence that hypnosis can lead to useful as well as more accurate information coming out. Provided it is carefully used, it does seem to have a place in the legal system. However, a relatively new way of obtaining more information from witnesses is now in common use in several police forces. It is called the cognitive interview, and it involves a number of different techniques.

1. Witnesses are told to report everything and not to make judgements about what is important.
2. Witnesses are told to try to picture the exact scene. Sometimes the police re-enact a crime in the hope that this will prompt memories, and there is some evidence that taking witnesses back to the scene of an event does lead to their recalling more information.
3. Witnesses are asked to recall events in a different order from the way they witnessed the events by, say, remembering the incident backwards.
4. Witnesses are asked to recall using the viewpoints of say the burglar, or the person being mugged and so on. This method seems to work better in children than in adults.

A large number of studies has shown that this procedure can increase the number of accurate memories of a witness by anything up to 40 per cent, without increasing the amount of incorrect information. More recently, the originators of the cognitive interview have improved it by training interviewers in interviewing techniques. Clearly things can be done to increase the chances of law-breakers being brought to justice.

Advice to the Jury

Our experience is that those who are selected for jury service take their responsibilities extremely seriously. The jury has to balance the dangers of sending an innocent person to prison against the rights of victims of crime to see justice is done, and a mistake either way is a disaster. Yet, as you will have seen from what has been said in this chapter, the task of getting it right is very difficult, because so many things affect the accuracy of evidence and so many commonsense ideas, such as relying on eyewitnesses' confidence, may be dangerous. Add to these problems the fact that jurors are not encouraged to take notes during the trial, so they may not be able to remember accurately what has been said. Fortunately things are not as bad as they might appear.

In many situations there is corroborating forensic evidence to support the statements of eyewitnesses, and clearly the combination of the two is very important. In other situations a number of different factors come together to make eyewitness identification more reliable – the suspect had a limp, a funny way of swaying when he walked, was always saying a particular word in a particular way, and so on. It must be remembered that we usually recognize an individual by a number of features, not just the face, but posture and voice, as well as a range of different memories. Again, while it is important not to rely on witness confidence in isolation, especially when dealing with an event involving strangers, there is often evidence to support a witness's confidence, although, of course, they may still be wrong in relying on other factors – many people walk with a limp, for example.

Courts could help jurors much more by taping or videoing the proceedings and letting the jury have a copy. That would make it possible to check in the jury room disputed questions over what was actually said. Judges seem to assume that their summing up is all that is needed, but in our experience jurors often find it impossible to remember all the major points in summing up, and it is, in fact, often delivered in such a boring manner that jurors find it difficult to concentrate.

The present legal system means that we have no choice but to use eyewitnesses. It is not perfect, but it is much better than any alternative. What we can reasonably ask is that, as more psychological knowledge becomes available to help improve the system, it is adopted. The law is too serious a matter to be left to the legal profession.

In summary, memory is a key part of our legal system. We use the memory of eyewitnesses to decide if an accused is guilty or innocent. Unfortunately, a great deal of research has shown that under some circumstances eyewitnesses may not be accurate, even though they think they are. What happens after an event can affect an eyewitness's memory for that event, for example, so that identification parades are often flawed. A number of steps can be taken to improve identification parades, and these are outlined in this chapter. On the positive side, research has shown how the use of a technique called the cognitive interview can help the police to get more accurate information from eyewitnesses. Research in many areas is going on, and the hope is that this will improve legal procedures even more.

14

Memory in Children

Understanding a Child's Memory

The memory of young children is not as good as that of adults, and there are several reasons why this is so.

1. Adults are better than children at using memory aids, such as rehearsal, which help memory.

2. Adults have a greater knowledge to start with than children, and the greater the previous knowledge, the easier it is to remember new information on a topic.

3. Adults understand much better than children how their memories work.

4. Children are sometimes less willing to try to remember.

Using Memory Aids

Adults use a large number of ways of improving memory, including many of the methods discussed in previous chapters. An adult, for example, knows that repeating something to him- or herself can make it easier to remember at a later stage, although just repeating something over and over again, without thinking about it, is not as effective as thinking about what is being repeated. Even though many young children do use some memory aids, such as rehearsal, some of the time, they are not very good at it. Learning to use rehearsal seems to increase between the ages of five and eleven years old. Children can be seen to move their lips more, as they grow older, when they are trying to remember, say a list of words. This is a strong indication that they are using rehearsal more as they grow older.

Another strategy that does not seem to be used as much by young children is linking together words that they want to learn. For example, if an adult needs to link the words 'telephone' and 'calculator', he or she may perhaps picture themselves using the telephone as, say, a calculator. A young child is more likely to repeat the words together or, in the case of a very young child, to do very little.

The use of memory aids is not something that is absent in children but present in adults; rather, it is something that develops throughout life. Many adults are not aware of using memory aids, such as imagery and first letter prompting, that can help them in a whole range of memory tasks from remembering faces and names to remembering words in a foreign language or remembering points to be made in essays. It is not so much that we develop an ability to use these memory aids as we mature. It is clear that we learn about them through the educational system and from our friends and our own reading of books such as this one. Useful ways of improving memory can be taught to children, of say, six years old and over, and there is evidence that German parents spend more time teaching their children about memory and studying methods than do parents in the United States, for example. We will talk about teaching children about memory aids later in this chapter.

Understanding How Memories Work

Children do not use memory aids and memory methods as well as adults. What is more, they do not understand as well as adults when they should use them, so even if children are taught to use memory aids for one task, they are less likely to use them again for another task than are adults. Of course, even adults are not always good at knowing about memory aids and when to use them. Many people reading this book will have picked up hints on how and when to use memory aids – if they already knew about them, there would be no point in reading this book! It is not that children cannot learn about memory aids and when to use them – as we noted above, this can be done through parents and schools – it is that adults appreciate more how their memory system works.

Children, for example, are overconfident about what they can remember, compared to adults. Even when they fail to remember as much as they think they will, they are confident they have good memories and will remember better next time. Not only are they over-confident about how well they are going to do, they are, on average, over-confident about how well they have done in a memory test! Many parents have had the experience of being assured by their child that they knew their work, only to find that they have failed in exams. Nor do children always seem to learn from experience. Not, it should be emphasized, that adults are perfect either! There also seem to be gender differences, too, with young girls being less confident – and therefore more realistic – than young boys about how good their memories are.

As with any skill, children are likely to take longer to learn memory skills than adults, but it has been shown to be useful for children to learn memory skills, just as it is useful for adults. However, it is essential not just to teach children how a memory aid works or how to use a memory aid; they must also be taught when and when not to use the aid. In other words, when teaching children how to use visual imagery to learn lists of unrelated words, the knowledge will not be used again unless the child is shown exactly how this method can be used for other tasks, such as name–face association, language learning, remembering shopping lists or whatever.

There is, however, one major advantage of getting children to use a memory aid to learn a list of words, just for its own sake, especially children who are not progressing as well as they should. For many people, being able to recall, say, seven or eight words out of ten using the peg method shows them that they are capable of remembering large amounts of material, if only they would use memory aids. Instead of lists of words, learning five or six words in a foreign language rapidly has the same effect – that is, giving the individual confidence that the problem is not a lack of ability but a lack of 'technique'.

This method of improving confidence does not work for everyone because a few people find imagery difficult, and some people are so lacking in confidence that they do not try properly to make an image. Using this method to increase a child's confidence, therefore, has to be approached with care. Do not raise expectations in your child that he or she will do well. Present it as a task that works for some people, but not for others, and don't regard it as a 'failure' if it does not work for your child. But even if one task does not produce any gain, it is still important to talk to your child about a range of memory aids and preparing for exams. Teachers often do this but not necessarily in a way that is useful for your child. It should be remembered that it is as important that your child has confidence in his or her abilities to use memory aids as it is to know how memory aids work.

One way of showing your child – and indeed yourself – that memory aids are effective is to compare how well you do in a memory task without using a memory aid and how well you do when you do use a memory aid for the same task. You can do this by getting your child to learn a list of, say, ten foreign words without using key words, then to use key word images to learn the same list of words. Most people are convinced by this kind of demonstration that memory aids are very helpful indeed.

Some Memory Tasks for Children

Spelling
One of the big problems in learning English is that there are so many exceptions to the rules, and the rules themselves do not seem logical. It is no wonder that we often find it difficult to spell correctly.

However, it is possible to teach your child (or yourself) to overcome some of the worst spelling problems by using simple memory aids. You do this in three stages.

1. Find out what spelling errors the child makes frequently and list them.
2. Together with your child, make up a memory aid for each word and make sure that your child gets the spelling correct when he or she uses the memory aid.
3. Give no more than five such words in any one session, but go over the words from previous sessions frequently in order to make sure that the correct spellings are remembered.

You have to make up a memory aid that easily links the problem part of the word to the memory aid. Here are some examples, taken from personal experience.

Across – The error was spelling the word 'accross'. Remember there is only *one sea* across to America (one 'c').

Carefully – The error was spelling the word 'carefuly'. *To hell* with driving careful*ly* – i.e., 'two "ll" with driving carefu*lly*'.

Their *vs* there – The error is to mix them up. Imagine thinking, '*EE, I* love *their* dog! *EE I* love what belongs to them! – i.e., if it doesn't belong, then it is not *EI*.

Historical Dates
Remembering dates is actually quite easy and involves applying the memory system that you learned in Chapter 3, the number–letter system. Suppose you wish to remember the following dates:

1745 (tkrl) Bonnie Prince Charlie and the Jacobite rebellion

1815 (tftl) Battle of Waterloo

1941 (tprn) Pearl Harbor

You translate numbers into letters and make up a word by using any vowels you like. In the case of most dates you can drop the 1 – *1*745 becomes 745, for example, but you will still remember the date.

> (1)745 becomes k r l – e.g., 'coral' (sounds like k here) Bonnie Prince Charlie's rebellion
>
> (1)815 becomes f t l – e.g., 'fatal' (Waterloo)
>
> (1)941 becomes p r t – e.g., 'port' (Pearl Harbor)

You can then imagine Bonnie Prince Charlie fighting at the OK Corrall (it is the K sound that matters), Waterloo being fatal for Napoleon and sailors in port as Japanese planes attack Pearl Harbor.

Remembering dates and who did what is, of course, a good way to organize points you want to make in a history exam. You can link dates and people with, for example, the peg system so that you increase the likelihood that names and dates, and therefore events and their causes, will be remembered in a way that helps you to answer an exam question.

Learning a Foreign Language

As we saw in Chapter 4, using imagery can help you to pick up a foreign language vocabulary. Older children and most adults find it useful to make pictures in their mind's eye and this process makes certain that learners have to try actively to learn the words. However, for young children and those adults who have difficulty making a picture, it is probably best to provide some help in the form of pictures which link words together.

A parent, for example, can draw a picture with a child, so that the child is actively involved in creating the link. Even children of six or seven years of age have been shown to benefit from the use of the key word method in language learning. Of course, there is no real substitute for immersing a young child in the foreign language to be learned by taking them abroad and letting them mix with children who do not speak their own language. There is some evidence that young children in this situation are better able to pick up a new language than anyone past the age of puberty.

In summary, young children do not, as we have noted, have the same memory skills as adults. Memory skills develop over time as a result of education and experience, and young children can remember less at one 'go' than adults. They also tend to be over-confident about how good their memories are. It does not appear that, in one respect at least, children are better at remembering than adults. Young children who have to move to another country and learn another language seem much better adapted to doing this than adults. However, children are able to benefit, as are adults, from many of the memory aids and methods discussed earlier, and skills like spelling can be helped with memory aids.

Memory in Later Years

Many aspects of memory decline with old age, but not all of them do. Older people are just as good as younger people at remembering incidents from their past lives, and they are also often better if they have a well-established skill, such as languages or chess, than a younger person who is not so skilful.

Some memory skills do begin to fail with age. One of the main problems is that, as we get older, we slow down in everything, including the speed at which we can take in new information. For this reason older people do not learn new material as easily as younger adults. This does not mean that older people cannot learn new things. It means that, other things being equal, they do not learn as quickly as younger people. But an older person fluent in French, say, will still learn new vocabulary more rapidly than a young person who is not fluent.

Another problem as one gets older is finding words stored in memory. Older people, for example, take longer than younger people to find a word when they are given a definition, such as 'What is a piece of land that is almost an island?' – a peninsula. More important, older individuals suffer much more from the tip-of-the-tongue phenomenon, where they know a word but cannot get it back. One study, which compared older and younger people, found seven times the number of tip-of-the-tongue experiences in the older group, and older individuals report that not being able to remember the name of someone they know is an increasing problem as they get older.

Younger people in a tip-of-the-tongue state often report a word that keeps coming to mind that disrupts the word they are looking for. An example of this from one of the authors is when he kept coming up with Emma Hamilton (Lady Hamilton), when he was trying to think of Emma Nicholson (a British Member of Parliament). Older people, however, find that instead of another name coming up, their minds usually go blank.

For most older people, the memory problems they get are not important and are probably not all that different from the problems that younger people get, although they probably get more problems. The names and things that people forget are almost always to do with people who have not been around for some time or the names of authors or characters of books that have not been read for a few years. Sometimes the name of a face that is familiar is not remembered because you meet the person in an unusual context. One of the present authors did not recognize his own mother when he met her on a train in London. She lived 400 miles away and he had no idea that she was in London. The face was familiar, but the context was so unexpected that he was not sure it was his mother! Fortunately, she recognized him!

One reason older people might think their memory is poorer than it is, is that failing to remember someone you feel you ought to remember is embarrassing. The failure implies that the forgotten person was not important enough to remember. Everyone gets embarrassed when this happens, and older people may be more affected than younger individuals because it is likely to happen more frequently. The solution is simple – just apologize and explain you are getting older! Of course, the older you get, the more people you will have met in the past, and the more chance you have of forgetting names – it is hardly your fault! It is very important that older people are not discouraged from interacting socially because of difficulties in remembering. There is considerable evidence that an active social life preserves memory.

Helping Memory as You Get Older

Is there something that can be done to help memory as you get older? Of course there is! You can use many of the methods that have been described in this book, and many studies show that memory aids can help older people. One study, for example, showed that using the key word method helped older individuals to learn a Spanish vocabulary. Another study showed that using visual imagery helped older individuals learn the names of people, and that this memory lasted for at least six months. Another study showed that training older people to review appointments every day at the beginning of the day meant they were better able to remember future appointments. They may not work as efficiently as for younger people, but they do work.

The real message for older people is not to worry too much about your memory. It does get less efficient as you get older, but so does your body. Just as you realize that you can't run for a bus as you used to do, so you cannot remember quite as well either. But not being able to run for a bus does not mean that you cannot walk to the bus stop and get around as much as before. It is the same with memory for most people. Just because your memory is less efficient than it used to be does not mean that you cannot operate just as well socially as anyone else. A great deal of research demonstrates that our memory improves in certain ways with age. People get increasingly better at learning and remembering knowledge that concerns their occupation and favourite hobbies. Also, research indicates that people do increase in wisdom with age. For many older people, the wisdom of age more than compensates for most memory lapses, which everyone accepts in any case. As was mentioned earlier, it is essential that older people enjoy an active social life in order to maintain their memory. One recent study has shown that elderly individuals who took acting lessons and performed in plays, had higher performance in unrelated memory tasks.

Real Memory Problems

Forgetting the name of an author or of someone you last met briefly several months ago is not a real memory problem. However, as one gets older, some factors do make it more likely that memory will be badly affected. Health, life experiences, such as bereavement, and social isolation can all have the effect of causing major memory problems.

Physical Health

A number of health problems have been shown to affect memory. Among these are high blood pressure, diabetes and arthritis. It is not surprising that chronic pain is likely to affect memory, since it is likely to affect concentration, and you are not likely to remember what you do not concentrate on. Even more important, chronic illness is likely to be related to chronic depression, and depression is a major factor in reducing memory ability in the elderly, as it is in anybody. Clearly, keeping as healthy as is possible, by good diet and exercise, is likely to lead to better memory.

Mental Health

As mentioned above, one of the most important factors that unfortunately tends to increase with age is depression. This can come about because of a large number of life events, including bereavement, job loss, chronic illness, divorce, social isolation and poverty. Of course, depression occurs at all ages, but some life experiences, such as losing a partner or chronic illness, are more likely to happen to older people. The effects on memory can be extremely bad, so bad in fact that the major symptoms of depression can be mistaken for Alzheimer's disease.

People who are depressed cannot concentrate on the world around them, and they cannot put enough effort into trying to search in their memory store for what they want to remember. The more they fail to remember what they want to remember, the more they believe their memory is failing, and the more depressed they may become. They will get into a vicious circle of not trying to remember, because they don't think they will be able to.

There are three major points about depression in the elderly. First, it can often be reversed, unlike Alzheimer's disease. Second, some medication that is used to treat depression actually can make memory problems worse. Third, it can sometimes be mistaken by doctors for Alzheimer's disease.

The treatment of depression is, of course, a highly complex matter, which requires expert medical help. At its earliest stages, family and friends can help considerably. For example, after a bereavement the family must try to make sure that the one who is left does not become socially isolated themselves. It is important to get people to talk about their problems and to seek ways of solving them. The American psychologist, Vernon Mark, gives an example of an elderly individual who started to have memory problems as a result of the stress she was put under trying to pay large bills. The reduction in stress and anxiety that came with solving this worry by getting in touch with the creditor effectively solved her memory problems. Of course, most depression cannot be solved as easily, but the example does illustrate that it is sometimes possible to tackle life stresses of elderly individuals by looking for and then seeking to solve a threatening life event.

When depression is severe, clearly other methods have to be applied, including psychotherapy and drugs. Mark makes the point that some anti-depressant drugs increase memory problems, while others do not, and he argues that Prozac appears to have no detrimental effects on the functioning of memory. Of course, all drugs can have harmful side-effects, but when anyone is being prescribed drugs for depression, it is a reasonable question to ask the doctor about the availability of drugs that may not induce memory problems. It is also worth remembering that a variety of drugs for a number of conditions, not just depression, can damage memory. It is always worth investigating whether any drugs that are being prescribed might make memory worse.

Alzheimer's Disease

One of the most common worries affecting people as they get older who notice that they are becoming more forgetful is that they are in the early stages of Alzheimer's disease. This disease of the brain affects not only memory, but personality as well. But it is very important to stress, first, that most forgetting as one gets older in no way resembles the forgetting seen in Alzheimer's disease, and second, some conditions, which are reversible if properly treated, have symptoms that are very similar to Alzheimer's, and these must be positively ruled out before a diagnosis of Alzheimer's is made.

As we have already noted, forgetting the names of people you met briefly last week, or of friends you have not met for a year or two, or of people you meet in unexpected places or ways, happens all the time to people of all ages. In no way is this a symptom of Alzheimer's disease. Forgetting where you put your keys, or the 'safe place' you put some money, or where in the car park you left your car is completely normal. Coming back from a shopping trip and finding that you have forgotten half the things you want to get is also normal at any age. All these things might happen more frequently as you get older, but they do not, repeat *not*, in any way mean that you are showing any signs of Alzheimer's disease.

What is more worrying is if someone tells you something, then two minutes later tells you the same thing as if he or she had not told you a few minutes earlier. One or two incidents of this kind are not important and sometimes everyone repeats something a second time for emphasis or even because they have forgotten that they have already told you. However, if this happens frequently, and the same thing is said several times in a short space of time without any indication that the person realizes that he or she has said the same thing before, it is a worrying sign. If, in addition, the same individual has such a poor memory that he or she cannot function socially – perhaps he or she does not remember close relatives and friends, or cannot cope with money or shopping, or he or she no longer has any sense of time, or forgets where the toilet is and so on – the symptoms clearly need serious investigation. But they may not be the result of

Alzheimer's. They could be caused by severe depression or other illnesses. It is vital that these alternatives are checked. It should be stressed, however, that a medical diagnosis of Alzheimer's disease is correct in the great majority of cases, but mistakes are possible if further testing has not been carried out to eliminate other possibilities.

Even if a diagnosis of Alzheimer's disease is made, this should not be the end of the story. New research is showing that some aspects of learning are still possible, even in Alzheimer's patients, especially in the earlier stages. Motor skills in particular seem to be teachable, so that toilet-training and washing and dressing seem capable of being taught. Some Alzheimer's patients have such well-developed skills in some areas that these last well into the illness. Mark describes one Alzheimer's patient who could hardly talk but who was a highly competent gardener, while another, who could not find his way from the bathroom, made good investment decisions.

It should be remembered, too, that research is going on all the time, not only into medication but into ways of helping Alzheimer's patients make the best of what they have got. A recent study taught an Alzheimer's patient where to put her dirty clothing and how to get to the toilet on time. In another study, a wife who was suffering from Alzheimer's disease kept insisting that she had not had supper even though she had just finished her meal, and became angry when her husband refused to make her supper again. The psychologist suggested that as many clues as possible be left around to remind her that she had had supper. All the dinner plates were left on the table, and the wife was made to help with the washing-up. The strategy worked. In another study, Alzheimer's patients were helped by painting the toilet door a completely different colour from the other doors in the house.

These examples show that it is worthwhile looking at the environment of the Alzheimer's patient to see if it can be changed to give more *cues* to the sufferer to help with remembering. Readers with an interest in caring for Alzheimers patients are strongly urged to read the chapter on this topic by Camp and Foss (see Further Reading for details).

These may be small things in terms of learning, but they are very important to the relatives of those suffering from Alzheimer's disease. It must, however, be said that caring for an Alzheimer's patient is difficult, not only because of the day-to-day problems of memory loss but because of personality changes, too, and we would not wish in any way to minimize these difficulties. We also recommend that anyone who has an elderly relative suffering from memory problems should read Mark's book, *Reversing Memory Loss* (see Further Reading). See also Chapter 6 on memory and health.

There are, of course, any number of commonsense steps that can be taken to help someone whose memory is getting a bit worse with age. For example, make sure you always put your keys in exactly the same place. There should be a 'special' place for anything of value, not somewhere that is especially safe for each for each valuable item, otherwise sooner or later the person will forget where a particular item has been placed. If you drive to the supermarket, always try to park the car in the same place. If the car has to be left somewhere different, write down the new place or at least make a special mental note of where it is parked. Often people are unsure whether they have switched the heating off or left the television on before they go off on holiday. If this happens to you, make a special mental note by saying to yourself: 'This is Tuesday, 3 December and I am now switching off the TV.' If you are still worried 200 miles down the road, phone up a neighbour who has a key – just to make sure. But if you pay attention when you are switching appliances off, it will not be necessary.

In order to remember to do things, a simple but effective solution is to keep a diary, and to make a list of things to do every morning. You must look at your diary every morning and look at your list throughout the day, but using these 'external' memory aids is very effective. Sometimes if you need to be reminded to do something at a particular time, it is useful to have a watch that bleeps – even if it does annoy others occasionally.

Remembering to take medicine is a serious problem for anyone, but more so for older people. One good tip is to leave the medicine where you are going to be automatically reminded when to take it. For example, if you always make a cup of tea in the morning, leave your medicine on or next to the teapot so that, as you make your tea, you have to move your medicine. As we saw in Chapter 9, special pill boxes are now available that mark out what pills should be taken every day, and these are very useful. Another useful idea is to leave messages around the house to remind yourself what you have to do. A friend or relative can do this, for example, by leaving notes stuck to prominent places, reminding the person to put out the dustbin because it is Wednesday.

A number of studies have found that if elderly people are familiar with their surroundings, they can cope generally quite well. Problems arise when they are put in completely unfamiliar situations. For example, an elderly person might cope well with shopping if he or she is familiar with the local supermarket but might become confused in another shop, where the arrangement of shelves is different. Provided safety is not a problem, it is probably better to leave a person in his or her own home than to move him or her to a new environment, particularly if moving is accompanied by depression at being moved. This is, of course, a very complicated question, and not only the health and safety needs of the elderly person but also the needs of the carers must be considered. However, one worry about older people living on their own is probably exaggerated. Sometimes the trigger for deciding an older person needs to move into a home is that cooking is left on the stove and forgotten, thereby causing a fire risk. The worry is that the older person might be a danger to him- or herself. However, this worry is by no means confined to the elderly. One of the authors recently asked a group of about twenty young students if this had ever happened to them, and every one of them admitted that it had! Of course, it might well be that making a mistake like this is an indication of a major memory and coping problem, but of itself it does not mean that the person is a major danger – we might all be in care if this were the case. The circumstances of each individual have to be investigated and where desirable, alternative cooking arrangements, such as microwave ovens, can be used instead of normal cookers.

In summary, as we get older, it is inevitable that our memory is affected. In the majority of cases, however, memory failures are no more than a slight nuisance and embarrassment. Forgetting where you put your keys or the name of an old friend does not mean there is anything seriously wrong, and there are, as we have seen, things that can be done to help, including the memory improvement methods described earlier. One major problem that affects people more as they get older is depression, which can have a major effect on memory, but there are ways in which people suffering from depression can be helped. Of course, there are individuals who suffer from brain damage as a result of ageing, but even here in many cases some small steps can be taken to make life a little better.

Impairment of the Nervous System

16

Throughout time, memory disorders have troubled people. However, not all memory disorders are the same, and the memory disorder that affects one person may be very different from the disorder that affects another. In this chapter we will consider the major categories of memory disorder, before looking at the common problems within each category.

Everyone forgets, and from time to time everyone learns slowly. However, there are two differences between a person with a normal memory and a person with a memory disorder. The person with a memory disorder has many more memory failures, and will also tend to have memory failures that rarely occur for people with a normal memory.

Types of Memory Failure

To be counted as a recall failure, a person either does not answer or produces the wrong answer. Not answering and answering wrongly show different memory difficulties.

Suppose someone is asked to name the current President of the United States. If the person said that they did not know the answer, it might suggest that they had a memory problem. Most people know who is the current President. However, a person could still have a good memory and not be able to recall the President's name. Such a person could be distracted or not be at all interested in politics. A person could also have a good memory and not be able to recall the name simply because they did not know the President's name. Some people, for example, do not follow the news and do not know the name of a new President. To determine if a recall failure indicates a memory problem, it is necessary to ask more questions to better understand what this person knows about the President.

Now consider a person who produces a wrong answer. For example, suppose the person said – in all seriousness – that the President was Harry S Truman. We would immediately suspect that this person had a memory problem. Consequently, a wrong answer often indicates a memory problem more readily than does a recall failure. However, it sometimes depends on the exact nature of the wrong answer. For example, if the question was, 'Who was the first man in space?' and a person answered 'Armstrong', this answer would not indicate a memory problem since many people might not realize that the person's name was Gagarin.

A special kind of wrong answer is when a person gives an honest and complicated answer that is not true. This kind of error is called a confabulation. An example of a confabulation would be a person who answered that the President was Harry S Truman and added that President Truman had been to visit yesterday. You and I would recognize quickly that this person had a memory problem. Consequently, a confabulation indicates a memory problem more readily than a wrong answer or a recall failure. Confabulations occur in the later stages of some memory disorders.

Like recall failures, recognition failures occur in different ways. A failure to recognize a familiar object or person is sometimes called a 'miss' because the person has 'missed' recognizing the familiar thing or person. For example, if a person could not find his or her coat in a cupboard in which it was hung, the person has 'missed' recognizing the coat. An incorrect recognition of a new object or of an unfamiliar person as having been seen before is called a false alarm. For example, a person who accidentally puts on a coat that is similar to his or her own has made this kind of error. Just as a wrong answer is more revealing of memory problems than a failure to answer, a false alarm often indicates problems more readily than a miss.

Recognition failures are more serious than recall failures. If someone can recall something, he or she almost always can recognize it. However, failure to recall does not mean there will be a recognition failure. Usually, a person can fail to recall something and still recognize it.

People remember something because cues trigger memory. There are relatively few cues when we try to recall something. Thus, there are few cues to help us remember in the question 'What did Mary wear at the picnic?' Recognition involves evaluating many cues at the same time. For example, many cues are provided if the question is, 'Did Mary wear this plaid blouse at the picnic?' and the blouse in question is held up as the question is asked. A person who fails to recall may claim that given enough time he or she will remember the answer. The same claim can be made with recognition but is less believable. A person who needs more than a few seconds to study the blouse will probably never recognize whether it was worn by Mary at the picnic.

Failure to recall certain information may indicate a memory disorder. A person may be asked to give the name of his or her spouse. Failure to recall the spouse's name suggests a serious memory loss, but a failure to recognize one's spouse indicates an even more serious memory loss.

The Memory System

The memory system is, of course, located in the brain. It exists throughout the cortex and in what is called the brain stem, which is at the top of the spinal cord. As with other parts of the brain, the memory system receives information from the senses and sends signals to our muscles, so we can respond with speech or movement.

Different types of memory are located in different parts of the brain. People who have suffered brain damage in a certain area, such as might result from a motor accident, may lose memory abilities. If the left side of the brain is damaged, the person may have great difficulty in learning abstract concepts and yet may be able to learn motor skills. If the right side or the back of the brain is damaged, the person may have difficulty with recognizing what is seen or heard. Although many memory functions reside in the brain, the precise location in the brain of many memory functions has yet to be discovered.

When memory fails us, it does so in one of three ways. We can fail to register something initially in memory, or we can fail to store over time what was successfully registered, or we can fail to retrieve something, despite successful registration and storage. We know this because although we often cannot remember something at the time we are asked, we manage to remember it later. Many psychologists assume that memory consists of several components, each with its own specific job to do. Much like a CD music system, each component of the memory system contributes to the overall functioning of the system.

Types of Memory Disorder

Forgetting events that a person once easily remembered before a disorder, such as brain damage following an accident or a stroke, is called amnesia. Not being able to remember events before the accident is called retrograde amnesia. Inability to remember events that occurred since the accident is called anterograde amnesia. A victim of a car accident may have retrograde amnesia for events that occurred just before the accident; the same person may also have anterograde amnesia for events since the accident.

Memory loss is often specific to certain kinds of information. Sometimes there is a loss of language skills – aphasia – which occurs because the person cannot remember words or combinations of them. Another memory problem is an impairment of movement of a person's arms, legs or body – apraxia – which may be due to forgetting how to move in certain ways. Sometimes there is an inability to recognize objects – agnosia – which is not due to difficulties in seeing but in remembering what the objects are.

Some memory disorders are identified by the pattern of memory problems. A sudden loss of speech and failure to remember anything new signal a stroke. A gradual loss of memory for new events often reveals Korsakoff's syndrome caused by diet deficiencies and/or alcoholism. A gradual loss of memory for new events and a progressive loss of memory for language characterizes Alzheimer's disease, while memory failures for new events and a decrease in the amount of speech often indicates deep depression.

The reason that different disorders produce different kinds of memory problem has to do with the make-up of the memory system. As we noted, the memory system is located in the brain stem and the cortex, and different parts of the brain stem and the cortex are responsible for different memory functions. These functions include a memory for what our senses register, for short-term memory processes and for long-term memory. Long-term memory includes information about language, events and things we have learned how to do. Finally, an executive system coordinates the different kinds of memory when we perform various tasks.

Different disorders result in different memory problems because different disorders involve damage to different functions. Amnesia for new events involves a defective ability to hold material for more than a short time, and amnesia for older memory alone occurs because long-term memory is defective. Some memory defects occur when there is a defect in the language memory. Some are due to a defect in those parts of event memory concerned with sensing objects. Some memory problems involve forgetting how to do things with the hands, and various kinds of memory problem may indicate that the coordinating mechanism is defective, also. Confabulation, recalling a complicated and false answer to a question, is the result of a defective coordinating mechanism. The middle and later stages of the dementia, such as senile dementia, involve a loss in this mechanism.

Finally, it is important to realize that memory problems sometimes arise temporarily. Memory performance can fluctuate from day to day or week to week simply because of many temporary factors: a change in physical condition due to lack of sleep or poor health, or a change in medication, emotional state, motivation and confidence can all affect memory. Temporary decreases in memory performance do not necessarily indicate a memory defect, and anyone's memory can noticeably worsen because of these factors and then get better again as the conditions change. Thus, when memory failures are on the increase, it is worth considering whether they are due to a temporary factor before becoming too worried.

Treatment of Memory Disorders

The last two decades have seen a revolution in how to rehabilitate (make better or alleviate) a person who has suffered a loss in memory function. This revolution has been due to the origin of new health science, called cognitive rehabilitation, which aims to restore, at least partly, memory and other mental powers, often by making more use of memory abilities that have not been damaged by injury. Many innovations have been developed by cognitive rehabilitation specialists in order to treat impaired memory thinking.

Until just a few years ago, cognitive rehabilitation was available only in private hospitals and centres for medical research. In recent years, an increasing number of hospitals have established cognitive rehabilitation units to make use of the knowledge that has been developed. Cognitive rehabilitation units are available in many hospitals, although all too often patients are left to themselves within a year of an accident.

Cognitive rehabilitation may be helpful to a patient with head injuries. Patients with memory problems due to many other kinds of neurological impairment can also benefit from cognitive rehabilitation, including those with stress-related illnesses, alcohol dependency, drug addiction and even psychiatric disorders. Some methods of cognitive rehabilitation simplify troublesome mental problems that would otherwise cause confusion and anxiety. In some cases, these methods can enable a mildly impaired patient to improve existing thought processes. In other cases, professionals may teach occupational skills to patients who would not be able to acquire these skills from conventional education.

Cognitive rehabilitation theorists assume that memory rehabilitation is achieved by affecting one or more of the memory components discussed earlier. A patient may be taught mental activities that improve learning or remembering. Teaching the patient to adhere to better sleeping and eating habits can improve memory and thinking, while training in how to use appropriately designed devices, such as electronic memopads, which show on screen what is to be done when an alarm goes off, can enable patients to stick to a productive and satisfying daily routine. Even the teaching of certain social skills can give some patients more control over certain situations so that they can make better use of their somewhat reduced memory functioning.

Patients are encouraged to practice performing particular memory tasks, and the practice is typically supplemented with guidance on how to cope mentally with the memory demands of the task. In some cases the patient will be taught to make use of external memory aids, and patients with mild to moderate memory impairments can learn to improve their functioning in everyday life.

One of the problems of brain injury is that it often leads to attention difficulties. Approaches to helping brain-injured patients often concentrate first on improving attention. Once this problem has been overcome, approaches using memory devices and the 'whole-person' approach to memory rehabilitation have proved successful on many patients. Obviously, how helpful rehabilitation is likely to be depends on how severe the brain damage is. Since head injury invariably affects mood and usually leads to depression, memory-impaired patients often need psychotherapy. Sometimes the therapy can involve simple training in relaxation techniques, while at other times, individual treatment is needed to provide psychotherapy to combat depression.

At a minimum, cognitive rehabilitation can help patients to cope with the cognitive challenges of self-care. In some cases, it can help patients regain some self-sufficiency – meeting appointments, finding their way around a hospital, recognizing others, finishing acts that they start, for example – and in other cases, cognitive rehabilitation can help patients to recover sufficiently to qualify for vocational rehabilitation. Of course, there are some cases, such as in the last stages of Alzheimer's disease, when relatively little can at present be done.

In summary, different diseases and disorders produce different kinds of memory problem, and damage to different parts of the brain stem and the cortex produce different memory functions. One kind of amnesia is due to damage to short-term memory, while another kind of amnesia is due to a defect in the connection between short-term memory and long-term memory, and a third kind of amnesia can occur because long-term memory is defective. Another kind of amnesia can involve a defect in memory for language, and a special kind of amnesia involves forgetting how to perform actions with the hands.

When people develop memory problems because of brain damage, they are treated by therapists who have specialized experience in rehabilitating memory. These therapists, called cognitive rehabilitation therapists, teach patients mental activities that improve attention, learning or remembering. Therapists teach patients to adhere to better sleeping and eating habits that can improve memory and thinking. They also teach them to use memory devices and the social skills needed to gain better control of their memory. Approaches to helping brain-injured patients often concentrate first on improving attention, and once this problem has been overcome, approaches using memory devices and the 'whole-person' approach to memory rehabilitation will be tried, and these have proved successful on many patients. At a minimum, cognitive rehabilitation therapy helps patients to cope with the cognitive challenges of self-care and everyday life.

17

Memory and the Workplace

A memory failure or series of failures in the workplace can doom a person's chances of promotion. Fortunately, the memory tasks that can cause trouble can be easier to identify and to correct in the workplace than in other social situations, such as when we get together with friends. The reason why memory problems at work are often easier to handle is that they are often predictable.

Becoming Aware of Memory Problems at Work

The first thing to do about memory problems in the workplace is to identify them. Once they are identified, examine your performance critically. A key time to learn about appropriateness is when you have just failed at a memory task. For example, we sometimes fail to learn a person's name, despite having heard it clearly when we were introduced. If we make a note that we failed to do so, we are more likely to take steps to avoid making the same mistake in the future. You can decide which mental activities will work best for you when you have to perform the memory task.

In addition to learning more about how to perform troublesome memory tasks, you should periodically attempt to identify and eliminate habits that hinder your memory performance. Some bad habits are fairly general and interfere with many kinds of task. Others are specific. Many of the bad habits involve going against the advice you have read in the previous chapters, such as not listening or not taking notes.

'Work is called work because it is not fun.' It is natural to come to dislike certain tasks at work and certain people, especially one's boss. Holding a memory task in low regard bodes ill for your performance of that task. Some people do not bother to memorize a list of components because they consider such detail beneath them, but unfortunately for them, knowing about the components can make them much more efficient at finding and recommending those parts. Also knowing the list will help you to keep them organized, and keeping components in a disorganized state shortens a worker's life by the amount of time that is wasted in trying to find something.

Many people tolerate fatigue before a memory challenge, but many memory failures occur because we are tired. People often avoid making or referring to a list when it would be so easy to let the list do the remembering for them.

Evaluating Feedback

Your reputation at work includes how you handle memory tasks. If your co-workers and especially your boss think you do not know much about certain kinds of information, you will never have a chance to specialize in this area. Also, the more that you are known to be poor at remembering different kinds of information, the less likely it is that you will be advanced to management.

It is important for you to examine what others say to you about your memory performance. If a co-worker's feedback about your memory does not square with your own impression of your abilities, but you suspect the person may be right, monitor your performance in the relevant tasks for a few weeks. Your performance during a period of self-observation will indicate whether you need to prepare specifically for a particular task. If the feedback does not square with your own impression, and you have good reason to believe the person is wrong, then disregard the feedback. Periodic assessment of performance by means of self-reports, other reports or a diary, for example, can help you better to assess your memory ability.

Remember that this can be expected to fluctuate from day to day and over time.

Critical Memory Tasks at Work

Each job requires you to know certain information. Make sure that you study this information, and familiarize yourself with everything to be learned before you begin to register information. Use more than one way of trying to remember the same material if possible – you might, for example, learn a list of items by first rehearsing the items, then by making judgements about whether each item is pleasant or unpleasant. Most experts believe that the use of different techniques leads to longer-lasting and easy-to-find memory traces.

Communicating When You are Called to Account

When your boss asks you to remember something that you are sure you can recall with enough time, recall at a relaxed pace. Hurrying will lead you to miss recalling parts of the information you really can remember, and hurrying is also more likely to result in inaccuracies than is slow, deliberate recall. If possible, try to delay giving your recall when the desired information is not yet available in your mind.

You should also recall in an order that is best for the information and presentation conditions. Start from the beginning and go through the sequence of events when you are trying to recall a story or an event. When information has been presented briefly and recently, recall the last information first, then the first information, and finally the information in the middle.

Check the content of what you have recalled in your own mind before you say it aloud. Is it consistent and plausible? If not, your memory may be flawed. Be sensitive to the fact that you can mistake the content. Initially, you might misinterpret the question or query posed for remembering.

Your recall can be in error in two ways. You can leave out something or recall something that is either not called for or something related to material just remembered. Correct memory for facts might be remembered out of sequence, at the wrong time – such as remembering an appointment after it was to occur – or in the wrong place – such as recalling information that is socially inappropriate. With continued attempts to remember, false memories can come up repeatedly, and these are often difficult to distinguish from the original memory. Finally, after retrieving part of the desired information, you may think you have finished remembering, when you are not actually finished.

Long-term occupational experience may lead to excellent memory abilities for job-related memory tasks. Thus, if you want a superior memory, you may have to practise memory tasks over a considerable period of time. You can no more expect to improve your memory skills by merely reading a book than you would your tennis or golf skills. Hard work and practice are essential. This is partly because our ability to remember many things declines over time – we get rusty on the foreign vocabulary we learned at school, or the maths we learned, unless we are using the skills regularly. If you know that sooner or later your knowledge of certain information will be challenged by a boss or co-worker, practise recalling what you will be challenged on. You can achieve a dramatic ability to recall important things just by practice.

If you know that a particular retrieval task occurs on many occasions, a sure way to excel at this task is to engage in remembering practice. For example, suppose you sell a line of products and you want to know all the different types or models. After you have learned to identify each product type, practise recalling them – without restudying. You might want to try some of the methods discussed in earlier chapters. Learning lists of products or names of clients, for example, is often helped by using these methods in the first place. Practice helps to keep the memory alive. Next, practise recalling the entire product line – all of them – again without restudying. Then practise recalling again, and again, until you are satisfied with your improvement. As we noted in Chapter 3, memory is helped if you gradually increase the time between practice attempts.

Remembering to practise is also very effective for enhancing retrieval of information you once knew well but now recall poorly. Many people find that their school French or Spanish comes back quickly when they have to use it on a visit to a French- or Spanish-speaking country. As if by magic, forgotten information comes back to life.

If, when you are at work, you expect to be called upon to remember something at a meeting about some topic that is now hazy, practice retrieving the topic several times beforehand. Even without any re-learning, you will recall more information and have faster access to it. By combining re-learning with remembering practice, you can further improve your performance.

Finally, remember to think about your physical condition and emotional state when you have to attempt a troublesome memory task. If necessary, decide on ways you can optimize your physical condition and emotional state on the occasion of the memory tasks. For example, some people get very anxious about failing to meet appointments. Appointments may have to be remembered when you are tired or anxious. Identify your likely condition at the time you will need to remember, and if you think that aspects of your physical condition or emotional state or attitudes or emotions might work against you, make sure that these factors are part of your memory plan. You can, for example, make sure you get a good night's sleep before a meeting – but avoid taking sleeping pills, because they may make you sleepy in the morning.

If you cannot practise out loud, alone or with someone you trust, practise recalling mentally. Mental practice is often used by professional athletes to prepare for sporting competitions, and it can further increase the usefulness of name-learning techniques discussed in Chapter 4, so that you will use them more efficiently. Mental practice can be used to create introduction tasks – such as imagining meeting people as they are introduced on a talk show – or asking a friend to pretend to invent names and go through introductions. Of course, not everything is difficult to remember. Where we are using the same tools or equipment every day, the practice effect is built in.

Remembering Appointments

People typically remember most of their regular appointments without too much effort – for example, doctor's visits, parent-teacher meetings, weekly or monthly card games (such as bridge or poker) – and without having to use an alarm. Regular meetings are forgotten much less often than are unique appointments. A one-off agreement to meet an old friend, an ad-hoc business meeting in a club or a spontaneous arrangement to buy something on a certain day are easy to forget after deciding on what is to be done. If you make only a single one-off, ad hoc or spontaneous appointment a year, you may remember it perfectly well, but if you make such 'irregular' appointments frequently, you will fail to remember them more often than regular appointments. Take care at work that you do not miss appointments with either your boss or your co-workers.

Professional Attitude

Your attitude plays a significant role in your memory performance at work. If you want to learn something and are excited by the task, it is likely to be much easier for you than for someone who finds the topic boring. In Chapter 5 we pointed out how much interest in a topic affected memory. If you dislike certain memory tasks, this negative attitude will translate into memory failures because you will not put as much effort into learning. Therefore, because a poor attitude affects memory performance, a key way to improve your memory performance is to improve these attitudes.

Most attitudes are deeply rooted, of course, and the origin of many of your attitudes lies in your upbringing and past experience. Therefore, many of your memory attitudes will have been held by you for a long time, and although it is not easy to change them, they can be changed. If we are to change our attitudes about learning or memory, we must understand the stuff that attitudes are made of. To begin with, attitudes are feelings, the feelings we usually have when we think about or encounter various people, events and tasks. Some of our attitudes about memory tasks are positive, and we like to perform these tasks – for example, some people like learning phone numbers and easily pick up a new one, and some people like to travel and quickly grasp directions given to them.

These different kinds of attitude are as follows:

- Your attitude toward your memory ability.

- Your attitude toward a particular kind of memory task.

- Your attitude toward the kind of information processed in a memory task.

- Your attitude toward whether or not memory ability is changeable.

- Your attitude towards whether or not *your* memory ability is changeable.

Is a good memory attitude one that applies to all memory tasks? Or should you fine tune your attitude to deal with different situations. Society has led us to believe that memory ability is like a muscle: a person's memory is seen as strong or weak or somewhere in between. People with a good memory are supposedly good in all situations, and people with a bad memory are supposedly bad in all situations. This account of memory ability is very popular, but it is completely false, because each person has many memory abilities and interests, so it is quite possible for someone to have a perfect memory for the day's football results and yet have a poor memory for new telephone numbers.

The present authors have often listened to a group of people complain about their memory. Almost always, the people will be unanimous in claiming that their memory is awful. One person will moan: 'Oh my memory is terrible.' Another will shake his head and say: 'Mine is just as bad.' A few people will even have arguments about whose memory is the worst. Full of pride, they say, 'Your memory is bad but not nearly as bad as mine.' When you listen to such a discussion about how defective a person's memory is, you would think that these people were talking about the same thing.

Possessing certain abilities does not guarantee that you will perform well those tasks relevant to those abilities. If you have not had much practice at a certain task, you will still not perform the task well. You might, for example, have inherited an ability to learn words; however, if you rarely tried to learn words, you would still not live up to your intellectual inheritance for name learning.

If you dislike the information you should know, you have got a problem. If you dislike aspects of your job to the extent you have difficulty learning what you need to know about the job, something has to change. You have to work out a way to view the material positively if you are to learn it. Fortunately, you can take steps to neutralize negative attitudes. If it is worth it to you, you can even change some negative attitudes into becoming positive. For example, if you dislike material to be learned for work or school, spend some time identifying the positive features of what you need to learn.

Even for subject matter you detest, you can usually identify something positive about it. It takes time to convince yourself that some material that you dislike will help you in the long run, but the amount of time needed to do so is far less than the extra time needed to study something you dislike. Let us repeat that: it takes less time to convince yourself to take a positive outlook on some material than the extra time you will need to study this material while you dislike it. Indeed, often people learn little or nothing at all about material they detest.

Do not forget to look at earlier chapters on memory improvement to see how memory devices and memory strategies might apply to what you need to learn in your job. Imagine what kind of things you can do to make yourself think positively, especially in situations where you are unhappy. First, it is common experience that the more you get to know and understand, the more interesting it gets and the easier it gets to learn even more. Second, the better the job you do, even in a place you don't like, the easier it is to get another job or to get people in your present job to treat you better. Finally, you will never know whether you are capable of learning a particular job unless you give it a go.

After everything else is considered, your memory ability in the workplace will depend on your memory habits. It is crucial that you have good self-control: start projects when they are supposed to start; keep a project going and make sure you finish on time. It will not help if you have difficulty making up your mind.

If you take on too many projects, you will not be able to keep track of everything that you need to remember. Don't worry too much about the details. Be sensitive when the situation calls for your strengths and your special ability to be creative. You have to maintain a good attitude. If you forget something, you cannot blame it on others. Do not let your own personal problems bog you down. On the other hand, remain confident and concentrate on what is important.

These habits are summarized below.

Habits of Living that Favour Your Memory in the Workplace

SELF-CONTROL

OVERCOME DIFFICULTIES IN STARTING

OVERCOME DIFFICULTIES IN CARRYING ON

OVERCOME DIFFICULTIES IN FINISHING

DELAY THE DESIRE FOR REWARD

MAKE UP YOUR MIND PROMPTLY

PROJECT MANAGEMENT

DO NOT SPREAD YOURSELF TOO THIN

KEEP YOUR EYE ON THE OVERALL PICTURE

KNOW WHEN TO USE YOUR STRENGTHS

KNOW WHEN TO BE CREATIVE

KEEP A GOOD ATTITUDE

DO NOT BLAME OTHERS FOR YOUR MISTAKES

AVOID WALLOWING IN YOUR PERSONAL PROBLEMS

MAINTAIN THE RIGHT LEVEL OF CONFIDENCE

(BASED ON R. J. STERNBERG, 1985)

In summary, this chapter has examined in depth how to improve your memory in the workplace. A lot of the success in the workplace depends on having good memory attitudes, including your attitude towards a kind of memory task, towards the kind of information processed in a memory task and towards whether or not memory ability is changeable. Attitudes can be changed, so you should change any negative attitudes you have about memory and you will see your memory improve.

The Owner's Manual

In order to take good care of your memory, the first thing you need to do is to know how it works and how it doesn't work! Knowing how it does not work helps to eliminate false expectations of your memory. Knowing how it works suggests ways to keep it working well.

How Memory Does *Not* Work

One really important thing to understand about your memory is that it does not work in any way like a tape recorder, recording exactly what you see and hear, then playing it back to you exactly as you saw and heard it!

The main difference between your memory and a tape recorder is that human beings relate what comes in to material they have already stored. We make sense of what we see, hear and feel, and even though we might forget what we heard, we can often give an accurate account of what it *means*. For example, you probably can't write down exactly what was said in any of the chapters you have read in this book, but you can probably give a good account of some of the main points in your own words. So, even though the exact words were lost, the meaning is stored. No tape recorder does this. As we have noted, it has been found that people interested in football remembered new football scores better than people not interested in football. But tape recorders are not interested in anything in a way that affects memory!

What Memory Is

Perhaps a better model than a tape recorder for memory, although it is by no means perfect, is a library. New information is processed, just as books are catalogued so that they can be found at a later stage and can be placed in the correct 'place' on the shelves. New information is then stored (placed on the shelves) and later, when it is needed, it can be retrieved (looked up in the catalogue to see where it is and then 'retrieved' later from the shelves). This means that new information is not just stored as it comes in, like a tape recorder, but processed and placed with other similar material. When we forget, therefore, it might be because we don't process new material properly (catalogue it), or it somehow gets lost from the shelf, or, even if it is on the shelf, we may not be able to find it!

Processing new information

In many of the chapters in this book we pointed out how important it is for remembering that new information is properly processed. If you do not pay attention to what is coming in, it will not be properly processed, but the amount of time and effort you take and the way you process new information are also extremely important. The more you think about new information, the more you actually rehearse it, the more you relate it to earlier experiences or relate different but new information to other items of information by many methods such as visual imagery, the more likely it is that you will be able to find that information when you need it. In fact, most of this book has talked about efficient ways of processing what you want to remember so that you can get it out of memory when you need it. However, what we have also shown is that knowing about these methods and how they work is not enough. You must also think about *when* you *should* use them, and *when* you *should not* use them!

Here are some of the main rules to keep your memory working well:

1. Pay attention whenever you want to remember. If you are reading a book, take notes of the main facts and stop when you get tired.

2. Put effort into what you want to remember by processing thoroughly. If you want to remember a face, for example, look for outstanding features and think about the characteristics of the person. If you are studying for an exam, think about what the material means and if possible relate what you are learning to what you have already learned. A large number of studies have shown that the depth to which you process material – that is, how much you relate new material to what is already stored – has a major impact on what you remember later.

3. Use effective memory aids for processing where appropriate.

Among the memory aids that have been shown to be effective in appropriate situations are:

1. The first letter mnemonic for exams (see page 92)

2. The key word method for languages (see page 36)

3. Visual imagery for names and faces (see page 28)

4. The digit letter system for numbers (see page 24)

5. The peg word system for a mental filing system (see page 13)

6. The peg word system for remembering jokes (see page 20)

7. The method of loci, peg word system for remembering speeches (see page 18)

It is vitally important that you test each of these systems out on yourself to see if they work for you. Nothing works for everyone, so if any of these does not work for you – don't use it.

Non-memory Factors

A large number of factors – illness, fitness, confidence, interest, certain kinds of substance such as coffee, glucose, drugs and so on – affect memory processing. Check with Chapter 8 to see how you can change your lifestyle to improve your memory ability, if that is what you need to do.

The Nature of the Material

How well you process new material does not just depend on what you do to it, it also depends on the nature of the material itself. If something is already meaningful to you, it is much easier to remember it than if it is meaningless. Read the following sentence once.

TA KOKEENA FASOLYA EENAH VROMEEKA

Close your eyes and try to remember it. Now read this sentence once:

THE RED BEANS ARE DIRTY

Close your eyes and try to remember it.

Which sentence was easier to remember? Most people say the second one, even though they mean exactly the same thing. The first sentence is a Greek translation of the second one! But of course, the second sentence is meaningful; the first is not if you do not know Greek! But the same is true for all memory tasks – the more meaningful the task, the easier it is to remember, other things being equal.

As we saw earlier, one study of football results found that if people knew a lot about football before the results come in, they could remember more results. This is because the results are meaningful to those who are interested in football and are effortlessly remembered. To those who are not interested, every result is an effort to remember!

Many of the memory aids we looked at in earlier chapters are aimed to make things more meaningful than they otherwise would be, even in an absurd way. Linking *cow* to the Spanish word *vaca* by picturing a cow with a vacuum cleaner, cleaning a field is at least something you can easily picture, however odd it might seem. Organizing things that go together in meaningful lists also makes use of the principle of making meaningless things meaningful. But, most important of all, the more you know about an area, the easier it is to link anything new to what is already known. When you first start to learn a foreign language, everything is new and difficult. The more fluent you are, the easier it is to remember the meaning of a new word. In any field of study, therefore, the more you study, the easier it becomes, to take in new related material.

Rate of Presentation

Because we are limited in how much we can take in at any one time, we sometimes cannot remember things because we are overwhelmed with new information. When this happens, we tend to remember the beginning and can usually remember the last part of what is new; it is the bit in the middle that tends to be forgotten the most. There are exceptions to this, of course. If something that you witness stands out as being very different, you will often remember this, but you often forget the details of what happened just before and just after.

One of the problems of using some of the memory aids in real life is that events take place too quickly for you to be able to deal with them 'on the spot'. For example, in order to remember that someone is called Mr Sykes, you have to think of a substitute word for Sykes, say socks, then picture Mr Sykes with, say, socks covering his ears. This takes time and it is difficult to carry on a conversation and make a picture at the same time. What you should do is to excuse yourself from the situation and make a mental picture when you visit the toilet or go for a drink. If you are trying to make sense of someone's lecture, the same problem arises. By the time you have thought of a way of remembering a point, three more points have gone by. Again, don't try to remember at the time. If you want to remember, note down the key points, and try to remember them later, in your own time.

Context

One interesting fact about memory is that we do not just remember what we are trying to learn about an event or facts. We also remember, without trying to, all sorts of other factors about what we are learning! One study has shown, for example, that if we learn a list of words in one room, we will remember more words later on if we are asked to remember these words in the same room we learned them in rather than in a different room. If we learn a list of words under the influence of alcohol, we will remember them better later if we try to remember them under the influence of alcohol than if we are sober! If we learn a list of words when we are sucking a sweet, we may remember the words better if we are sucking the same kind of sweet when we try to recall them later, compared to not sucking a sweet or sucking a sweet that tastes different! Obviously it is best if you can learn and remember in the same kind of situation.

There are at least two situations where these context effects are very important. It is a common experience that it is much more difficult to remember the name of someone you know when you meet unexpectedly in a new situation. Often older people worry that their memories are failing when this happens, but it happens to everyone and is not important.

A more important use of 'context' effects is in the case of eyewitnesses, when people are taken back to the original scene of a crime in the hope that it jogs their memory. One study of young children found that they remembered much more when they were taken back to a park where events had occurred, compared to just trying to remember from memory without going back to the park. Even if you cannot go back to the original 'event', it is often useful, when you can't remember where you have put something, to retrace your steps mentally, to go back to the point where you definitely remembered, say, coming to the kitchen with your keys – what happened then – the phone rang – you answered it – you took the phone back into the kitchen – then the doorbell rang – you put the phone down – the keys are where you put the phone down!

Why Do We Forget?

This is the $64,000 question of memory – why do we forget? If we did not forget anything, we would not need memory aids. Life might not be wonderful, though. We would drag up all our long-forgotten unpleasant memories, and we would remember things that were no longer of any importance just as easily as more important memories. But we do forget. The question is why?

At first sight the question seems simple, but it really is very complicated. We have already seen in earlier chapters that non-memory factors can make a big difference to remembering – how interested we are, how much attention we are paying, how much we make new information meaningful, and how much we already know about the subject. However, when we are dealing with new, meaningless information, our memory is usually limited. Read the following sequence of numbers quickly, just once.

8 3 9 7 2 5 6 8 4 1

The chances are that if you close your eyes and try to remember it, you will not be able to. For new, meaningless unrelated material, we seem to have a limit of some five to nine items we can take in at any one time. It has been suggested that this shows we have a limited short-term memory of about seven items. New material enters short-term or working memory, and if it is not processed quickly, it will be forgotten. If it is processed, such as by repeating the numbers, it will be transferred to the long-term memory, where it will be held for a long time – or so the theory goes. The trouble with this theory is that a great deal of what we experience seems to be remembered effortlessly, without having to be rehearsed. The problem does not seem to be in our lack of ability to store new information. Remember how much you could recognize after one reading in Chapter 1. The problem seems to be in finding the material once it is stored. In other words, a major problem in memory is in finding information once stored rather than in storing it. Again, we clearly process virtually all new information in terms of its meaning.

Read this sequence:

8 3 9 5 X 2 4 8

What stands out? Most people immediately say X. But it stands out only because we are categorizing words as they come in, in terms of their meaning. This means they enter long-term memory. They are not 'kept' in an isolated short-term memory store until being transferred to long-term memory. It is quite possible, therefore, that everything enters our long-term memory, and the reason we forget is that new information is much harder to find in long-term memory because it is not as well 'catalogued' as older, well-learned material.

It is possible, however, that we forget because what is in our memory store decays over time, rather like a piece of iron rusts if it is not used. It is difficult to believe that we store absolutely everything we experience for all time. The problem is, we can never know if that is the case, because we cannot tell whether something we cannot remember is no longer there because it has decayed, or simply that it is there, but we cannot find it. What we do know is that there are many occasions when we can make it easier to find memories in our memory store, by using a memory aid, for example. This shows that a lot more is stored than we can normally get out. Again, using other methods of searching our memory store, such as the first letter search strategy discussed in Chapter 11, also shows that if we use more efficient ways of looking for what is in store, we can often find it. This does suggest strongly that much more is stored in memory than we can normally get out at any one time. This means the memory is there – it is not lost by decay.

One reason we sometimes cannot find what we are looking for is that forgetting might be due to similar material being stored together, making it difficult to distinguish what we are looking for from other, similar memories. An analogy might be with telling golf balls apart. Suppose you take a new golf ball out of your bag. You will have no difficulty in picking it out as the golf ball you have just seen, but if you now take another identical golf ball out of your bag, put both of them in your pocket and shake them around, you will not be able to say which was the first ball you took out of your bag. The first ball has not disappeared, it is just not possible to distinguish it from the other, similar ball. Similarly in memory, the problem is not that the original memory disappears – merely that it becomes 'mixed up' with similar memories, so you cannot always tell which one you are looking for.

By processing each memory so it is unique, as we do with many memory aids, we make it easier to distinguish one memory from other memories in our memory store and so make it easier to get it back again. Interference, as this theory of why we forget is called, probably accounts for much of why we forget, but it is still quite possible that, over time, we do completely lose some memories from store because of trace decay and lose some parts of others. But the most important thing to emphasize is how much we can do to remember a great deal of information that we would otherwise forget. If we pay attention to new information, if we process it efficiently by linking it up to what we already know and if we search for it effectively, as we saw in all the earlier chapters, we can remember – not perfectly, not forever – but very much better than before. It is difficult to ask for much more!

How can I keep my memory in good working order?

What you cannot do, is keep your memory in good working order simply by practising to remember lists of new words. Memory is not like a muscle, which improves with exercise. On the other hand, it is also true that if you pay attention to what you want to remember, and how you should remember, then you will be able to remember much better a whole range of things that are useful in everyday life. Even practising what you need to remember can have its place. For example, going over a poem that you need to remember after you have learned it to perfection will help to keep it remembered. Going over and using foreign vocabulary and grammar some time after you have learned it, does refresh the memory. Anyone who has learned a language at school some time ago knows how it becomes rusty unless it is used, but how quickly it can be refreshed when it is used again. The point is that practising your old French will help you to remember French; it will not help your memory for old friends or poems or anything else.

To keep your memory in good order means putting into practice the things we have talked about in the course of the book.

1. Pay attention to what you want to remember.

2. Take an interest in what you want to remember.

3. Learn about how your memory works.

4. Learn how different memory aids will help you learn and remember different things.

5. Find out what works and what doesn't work for you.

6. Don't be afraid to use external memory aids, such as diaries and lists, if they help you deal with your memory problems.

7. Take care of the non-memory factors that have a major effect on memory, such as physical health, good sleep patterns and so on (see Chapter 6.)

8. Remember that having confidence in your memory is vitally important. Don't dwell on the few failures that stick in your mind, but think of all the things that you do remember every day, almost without effort.

This book has covered many of the most important things you need to know about memory in many everyday situations. If you have read everything that has gone before, you will by this time know just how good your memory can be.

Further Reading

Baddeley, A.D., Wilson, B.A. and Watts, F.N. (eds), *Handbook of Memory Disorders,* John Wiley & Sons, Chichester, West Sussex, 1966 (see particularly the chapters by N. Kapur, B. Wilson and R. West)

Camp, C. and Foss, J. in 'The Intersection of Basic and Applied Research', ed. by D. Payne and F. Conrad, L.E.A. Mahawa, 1966 (this chapter describes some recent research on patients suffering from Alzheimer's disease)

Gruneberg, M.M., Linkword Language Courses, Edge Publishing, Nailsea, UK/N.T.C., Lincolnwood Books, Illinois. USA, 1987–96

Gruneberg, M.M. and Morris. P.E., *Aspects of Memory*, vol. 1, Routledge, London, 1992

Herrmann, D.J., *Supermemory*, Blandford, London,1995

Herrmann D.J., Raybeck, D. and Gutman, D., *Improving Student Memory*, Hogrefe and Huber, Seattle, 1993

Higbee, K., *Your Memory*, Prentice Hall, New York, 1988

Mark. V. and Mark. J. *Reversing Memory Loss*, Houghton Mifflin, New York, 1992

Searlman, A. and Herrmann, D.J., *Memory from a Broader Perspective*, McGraw-Hill Co., New York, 1994

Index